Free To Be Nothing

Free To Be Nothing

by

Edward Farrell

A Michael Glazier Book
THE LITURGICAL PRESS
Collegeville, Minnesota

A Michael Glazier Book
published by
THE LITURGICAL PRESS

Typography by Phyllis Boyd LeVane

2   3   4   5   6   7   8   9

Library of Congress Cataloging-in-Publication Data

Farrell, Edward J., Rev.
      Free to be nothing / by Edward J. Farrell.
          p. cm. —
      ISBN 0-8146-5780-X
          1. St. Agnes Church (Detroit, Mich.)—History.   2. City churches-
    -Michigan—Detroit.   3. Church work with the poor—Michigan-
    -Detroit.   4. Church work with the poor—Catholic Church.
    5. Catholic Church—Michigan—Detroit.   6. Detroit (Mich.)—Church
    history.   7. Farrell, Edward J., Rev. I. Title. II. Series.
      BX4603.D4S283   1989
      282'.774—dc20   89-7643
                                                                            CIP

Dedicated to my Aunt Catherine,
Sr. Joseph Barnabas Spellman
Sister of Nazareth
as she begins her
70th year of Religious Life
1 May 1989

TABLE OF CONTENTS

Preface 9

Foreword 13

  1. Free for Community 15

  2. Free for Conversion 30

  3. Free to be a Disciple 39

  4. Free for Evangelization 52

  5. Free for the Prayer that Leads
     to Action for Justice 70

  6. Free to be Embarrassed by the Poor 90

  7. Free to Plunge into the Incarnation 99

  8. Free to Live the Call of Holiness 112

  9. Free for the Journey into Mature Faith 124

 10. Free to Dream the Dream of Jesus 136

Postscript 149

Preface

1. "Have this mind in you which was in Christ Jesus
who though he was by nature God
did not consider being equal to God
  a thing to be clung to,
but emptied himself
taking the nature of a slave
and became as humans are
and being as all humans are
he was humbler yet
even to accepting death
death on a cross."

Philippians 2:5

2. " . . . God cannot catch us
unless we stay in the unconscious room
of our hearts. *We must be nothing,*
Nothing that God may make us something.
We must not touch the immortal material;
We must not daydream tomorrow's judgment—
God must be allowed to surprise us.
We have sinned, sinned like Lucifer
By this anticipation. Let us lie down again
Deep in anonymous humility and God
May find us worthy material for His hand."

Patrick Kavanagh
Collected Poems

3. "There is in my heart this great thirst to recognize
totally the nothingness of all that is not God. My

9

prayer is then a kind of praise rising up out of the center of Nothing and Silence. If I am still present "myself," this I recognize as an obstacle about which I can do nothing unless He Himself removes the obstacle. If He wills, He can then make the Nothingness into a total clarity. If He does not will, then the Nothingness seems itself to be an object and remains an obstacle. It is not 'thinking about' anything, but a direct seeking of the Face of the Invisible, which cannot be found unless we become lost in Him who is Invisible."

"It is time to start unweaving the outer social self and stepping out of it into the joy of emptiness. We should in a way fear for our perseverance because there is a big hole in us, an abyss, and we have to fall through it into emptiness, but the Lord will catch us. Who can fall through the center of himself into that nothingness and not be appalled?"

Thomas Merton
Hidden Ground of Love

4. "I have immense faith in the prayers of the poor."
"... the most fundamental intuition of *unknowing* which was the first source of my faith and has ever since been my whole life."

" ... a genuine realization that this is my vocation, but that I have not yet found the way of being really true to it. Rock bottom: I don't know what is down there. I just don't know."

Thomas Merton

5. "To reach satisfaction in all,
        desire its possession in nothing
To come to possess all,
        desire the possession of nothing
To arrive at being all,
        desire to be nothing,
To come to the knowledge of all
        desire the knowledge of nothing."

John of the Cross

6. "All creatures are a mere nothing. I do not say that they are something very slight or even something, but that they are a mere nothing. All creatures have been drawn from nothingness and that is why their origin is nothingness."

Meister Eckhart

"Outside of God there is nothing but nothing."

Meister Eckhart

7. "Are you willing to be sponged out, erased,
      cancelled,
          made nothing?
   Are you willing to be made nothing?
       dipped into oblivion?
   If not, you will never really change."

D.H. Lawrence

8. "The experience of nothingness is a mode of human consciousness. It is often a kind of exhaustion of spirit that comes from seeking "meaning" too long and too ardently. It is accompanied by terror. It seems like a kind of death, an inertness, a paralysis.... Yet even more vivid than the dark emotions are a desert-like emptiness, a malaise, an illness of the spirit and the stomach ... the will to act collapses like ash."

Michael Novak

9. "No matter how the nothingness experience comes about, we need to recall how holy nothingness is, how it deserves our respect and attention, how nothingness needs to be allowed to be in our lives. Its presence will change us in unfathomable and surprising ways. We shall be recreated as everything is created, *ex nihilo*, from the nothingness.... Without making this connection with the nothingness from which we spring, we fail to appreciate how unique each one of us is and how unique every being with whom we share the cosmos is. We lose reverence for being."

Matthew Fox

"To want nothing is the only possible freedom."

Matthew Fox

Foreword

In June of 1979, Mother Teresa of Calcutta came to St. Agnes Parish to begin her second foundation in this country. To the thousands of people who flocked to the parish that weekend, she said,

> "What you are doing I cannot do and what I am doing you cannot do. But together we can do a beautiful thing for the city of Detroit."

As Mother Teresa was leaving the parish, someone remarked,

> "Her secret is that she is *free to be nothing. Therefore, God can use her for anything.*"

●

Everyone wants to be somebody, something. Few dare to remember that we have come from nothing because too many have a terrible unspoken fear that we may return to nothingness. In the affluent world the thought of becoming poor touches off a psychic panic. Yet more and more clearly, Christian people recognize that the Gospel invites and enables us to be poor.

In the words of Mother Teresa:

> "You have said 'yes' to Jesus—and he has taken you at your word. The Word of God became man, poor; your word to God became Jesus, poor. And so this terrible emptiness—deep poverty—and your 'yes' is the beginning

of being or becoming empty. It is not how much we really
'have' to give, but how empty we are; so that we can receive
fully in our life and let Him live His life in us. In you today,
He wants to relive His complete abandonment to His
Father. Allow Him to do so. It does not matter what you
feel, as long as He feels all right in you. Take away your
eyes from yourself and rejoice that you have nothing. Give
Jesus a big smile each time your nothingness frightens you.

This is the Poverty of Jesus. You and I must let Him live in
us and through us in the world. Cling to Our Lady, for she
too, before she could become full of grace, full of Jesus, had
to go through that darkness, 'How could this be done?', but
the moment she said 'yes' she had need to go in haste and
give Jesus to John and his family."

1

Free for Community

I had a dream! In 1957, when I was ordained and sent to the new northeast suburbs of Detroit, parish life was at its zenith. Within a few months, a hundred couples had become involved in a dozen Christian Family Movement groups; it seemed as if the Parousia could not be long in coming.

Ten years later in July, something did come in Detroit, but it was not the Parousia. A revolution—a violent one—erupted a few blocks north of St. Agnes Church, a revolution that left thirty-eight people dead and one third of the parish area burned and soon to be leveled. Half of the forty thousand population were left homeless and forced to relocate. St. Agnes soon became a Catholic "ghost" parish. In the next decade, it would dwindle to one hundred families.

In 1962, the Little Brothers of Jesus made their first and only foundation in the United States in St. Agnes Parish. Their silent and radiant presence was a foreshadowing of new models of the Church yet to be born. In the summer of 1964, I moved into a 101 unit apartment a block from the Little Brothers in an attempt to explore how a priest might minister to inner city unchurched people. The six weeks I lived there were exciting and fascinating. I was ministered unto perhaps more than I ministered. Yet, it was discouraging and over-whelming considering my expectations of drawing people into the church. I soon realized that I could spend the rest of my priesthood with the people of this hundred unit apartment and have little "to show" for it. I learned so much in these weeks!

Then, after eighteen years of seminary work, I was appointed pastor of St. Agnes Parish. At last, I had arrived for the "Revolution in a City Parish," but no one else showed up! So I began, as I had years earlier, going door to door introducing myself to people and welcoming them to St. Agnes.

Each Thursday evening, I went to dinner in the home of one of the families of the parish. A meal with a family can be a good introduction of a family to a priest. I soon learned, however, that when one hardly knows the other, the occasion becomes almost formal. Rarely is there enough time really to share with one another. I did not realize then that I was trying to do too much too soon, that I had too much enthusiasm and too little patience and that I was not personally responsible to get that belated "revolution" going. My people were wonderfully patient with me and let me run off in all directions at once.

When the old caretaker's home on the church property became available, it became a "House of Prayer." The people were invited to make use of it with the assumption that every parishioner would know how to take best advantage of their own House of Prayer! The last Saturday of the month was scheduled as a day of prayer. And some people did come! A Eucharist offered each Wednesday evening was attended the first six months by only Mr. Holland, the seventy-five year old sacristan, and myself until slowly, a few more of the faithful parishioners began to come to celebrate with us.

For advent, a parish brochure was prepared as part of an outreach program to the unchurched people of the area inviting them to find a home with us for Christmas. Every parishioner was offered an advent kit with ten brochures and ten contact cards. Thus St. Agnes initiated its ministry of friendship and hospitality, welcoming the neighbor and stranger to the parish community ... and, it was almost a total flop! Out of fifty kits and five hundred cards, only two or three cards were turned in. I had totally underestimated the level of fear and anxiety in the area, even in contacting neighbors on one's own block. Anonymity is one of the great problems of the inner city; yet strangely, it is also a form of security and protection. Letting go of protective barriers and becoming vulnerable to a stranger is not easy.

Yet this first evangelization thrust was not a loss. An unusually quiet parishioner distributed her ten brochures and came back for a hundred more, and then for still more until, all by herself, she visited one thousand homes and apartments in the parish! What a joy to be learning to be "confounded"!

Although interest and concern for evangelization continued to grow in the parish, preparation and training were lacking. A first step in that direction came as a dozen women from the parish in two's and three's made the Cursillo intensive weekend and were ready to share that experience with others. Then Bishop Peter Birch of Kilkenny Island, Ireland came to visit St. Agnes along with Sr. Stanislaus Kennedy, the Executive Director of Kilkenny Social Services, to observe the programs and to share their experience. Sr. Stanislaus wrote of their visit to us:

> "I come out with one very clear picture of the *sign* of welcome and love and care and concern which exists in St. Agnes already. All those I met around the house and the church were such caring and concerned people that *that* in itself is a Sign. I think it is the extension of the Sign (the visible sign of Christ's unity and love) that is almost impossible to say what you should venture into first, but one thing I do know, whatever is done must be done exceedingly well. If it to be truly a Christian Service it must be a service *par excellence*. That does not mean that we must wait until we have the best instruments (because in that case we might wait forever); but whatever we do, it must be done with such love and care and concern to detail, that it must and will stand out. It must be, above all, very personal and a service which gives dignity, freedom and choice.
>
> "I think we also need to make explicit why we are doing this work and who we are speaking for. And we all need to be reminded often that we have a contribution to make. This is the great thing about Christianity, it accepts the smallest personal contribution and, by doing so, raises its value both as a *material* contribution and a *spiritual* contribution."

The day I was appointed to St. Agnes Parish, I heard that Mother Teresa of Calcutta was in New York. I phoned her and told her of my new assignment, the needs of our inner city and asked for her prayer for our parish. I suggested that if she ever were to make a second foundation in the United States, she might come to St. Agnes. Her response was "nothing is impossible with God." A little over a year later, in June 1979, I received a call from New York. It was Mother Teresa saying she was coming to St. Agnes the following week with three of her sisters for Detroit! To the thousands of people who flocked to St. Agnes that weekend she said, "What you are doing, I cannot do and what I am doing, you cannot do. But together we can do a beautiful thing for the city of Detroit."

An Intern Program in Prayer and Evangelization was developed by two Sisters who joined the staff that summer. Seven Religious Sisters and one lay woman from the United States and Canada responded to this program, staying with us an average of one month. Each intern was teamed with a parishioner so that the people were initiated into ministry with an experienced person. From the beginning, it was a mutual ministry. No project was initiated that could not be continued when the interns left.

As new horizons in ministry, evangelization and community continued to open up, we were compelled to recognize and articulate our conviction and mutual commitments. Daily Eucharist has become the core of our community and ministry, knowing that "without Him, we can do nothing," that He alone can empower and enable us to be "taken, blessed, broken and given." Each day begins with an hour of silent prayer in the parish chapel from 8:00 to 9:00 a.m. as a public manifestation of our prayer ministry for our people and the city. This invitation to prayer is extended to all people of the parish.

Members of the parish team committed themselves to a weekly review of life, sharing their inner lives with each other. Once a month, we focus on some form of community review of life, such as interpersonal relationships with one another. Often we "bump into" hidden unexpressed and sometimes unconscious expectations of one another and of the people we serve. We aim at a monthly day of prayer away from the parish for renewal and re-creation.

By the end of September 1979, St. Agnes Parish team had become a Basic Christian Community. The core community was composed of two Irish lay volunteer Social Workers, a religious sister and myself. The extended community involved four religious sisters, a Minister of Service and a laywoman parishioner.

We were ready now to develop long-term parish education and training. During Lent in 1980, Fr. Joseph Healey, a Maryknoll priest who had recently returned to the United States after ten years in Tanzania, was invited to lead an eight-day retreat on African Christian values. Alex Haley's "Roots" was still in the air. Each evening focused upon an African "root" that had universal meaning: community, waiting, familyhood, sharing, joint responsibility, faith, self-determination and the call to unity in action. For each value there was a Swahili code word, a short African story, an African proverb, a relevant Bible reading and suggestions for concrete action.

The presentation of African Christian values produced a wide spectrum of reactions and feelings. A good number of black Catholics were happy to rediscover African values that have meaning in contemporary urban America. One woman responded, "I thank you for bringing us 'the African Way.' It is very beautiful and is filled with deep human understanding. I always feel a spirit of kinship when I see a film of Africa. It is as if I were there, as if it is a part of me that is forever latent." Others did not see the relevance of their romanticized "primitive" African past and challenged Tanzanians to break out of their endless circle of poverty, low standard of living and lack of initiative. Some of the well-educated blacks considered the return to African roots as a step backwards, stressing that their roots are in American history and culture. In this setting of mixed attitudes and feelings as we searched and explored together, an unforgettable proverb echoed again and again, "I am because we are; we are because I am."

As the reflections moved deeper and became more personal, the people recognized that more and more Christians are called to be counter-cultural in our contemporary society. Truly to live Gospel values of community, sharing and mutual responsibility, we have to swim against the tide of American consumerism, individualism and intense competition. Gradually, the parishioners identified two specific values that have special meaning in their lives: risk and outreach. The people of St. Agnes are challenged to overcome the fear, suspicion and alienation in their neighborhoods by becoming vulnerable to others: opening our homes to visitors (including the needy stranger), telephoning the one who has given us a hard time, giving rides to travelers at night. Being Christian is dangerous. It might cost us our lives!

As the mission retreat drew to a close, a key conviction was the importance of a community response. Risk and outreach are not just personal responsibilities, but the mutual action of the whole parish. Outreach and risk happened! One member was supported in a protest against the negligence of a slum landlord; Christmas gifts were prepared for needy families in the neighborhood; prayer groups began to meet together with times for discussion and informal sharing; and, a group joined hands with an African Christian community in rural western Tanzania.

The revolution has not happened, but "small communities with a human face" have begun. As one parishioner said,

> "We are the mustard seed of the Archdiocese. And, we are already growing. We are experiencing a new trust, warmth and concern for each other. We are going to take more responsibility with the pastoral team for the parish. Evangelization is one of our priorities. We plan to reach out to the young, the old and all the unchurched people of our neighborhood."

Some of the projects that have come out of our thrust toward small Christian communities are:

CENTER FOR PRAYER AND EVANGELIZATION

This center, which began in 1972 at the Sacred Heart Seminary, has sponsored, each spring and fall, workshops such as "Second Career: Evangelization," "The Gospel in

Secular Life," "Evangelization: a Call to Faith, Hope, Love," and has been led by the staff and parishioners of St. Agnes.

NAZARETH HOUSE

On June 1, 1980, St. Agnes Parish opened Nazareth House, a center for prayer and evangelization, in the upper floors of its former convent. Based on urban parish spirituality, it centers on the Eucharist, meditative and contemplative prayer, shared faith in the style of small Christian communities and outreach to others through parish ministry. Over thirty individuals including priests, religious, laymen and women, single and married came to Nazareth House during its ten-week summer program from as far away as California. Most stayed for at least a week, eight for over a month. While here, they prayed, worshiped, shared faith and ministered with the people of St. Agnes. They visited the sick, the elderly and non-Catholic neighbors; they taught in our Bible School, played with our youth and dialogued with our poor. Most important was the faith and prayers they shared with parishioners, who came to spend time with the retreatants. And when they left, they understood in a new way the words of Revelation, "You see this city? Here God dwells among His people."

Nazareth House did not end with its summer program. It continues to attract men and women who wish to come and spend time in prayer in the heart of the city. Nazareth House has been a force in dispelling the myths of the city, myths of evil, of fear, of the poor, of people different from ourselves. As a movement toward reconciliation and peace, Nazareth House is a symbol and a complement to the courage, hope and faith of the people of St. Agnes.

SELF-HELP PROGRAM

On June 9, 1980, a Self-Help Program began with a thrift shop opening in the school as a means of supplementing the income of the helpers as well as a service to the local community. A small yet significant effort, we hope this will be an alternative to handouts, offering an opportunity for initiative and decision making.

ROSA PARKS COMMUNITY ARTS CENTER

June 14, 1980 saw the inauguration of the Community Arts Center with the help of a $30,000 Foundation grant. As an inner city arts academy, this new concept introduces the arts to a broad range of people. Classes in music, dance and art are offered to adults and children—the whole family. Recognizing the importance of fine arts education in everyone's life, the arts center is designed to reach people who are in need and have not had the opportunity to develop their own talent and to discover the cultural opportunities available in Detroit. Now a resident of our community, Rosa Parks is the black woman who refused to go to the back of the bus in Montgomery, Alabama and touched off the Civil Rights Movement.

MINISTRY OF OUTREACH

Two Sisters work full time in Social Service and Outreach at St. Agnes Church, which is centrally located. With a reputation for hospitality, people often stop in for a friendly visit. When they are in need, they seek help, and, at other times, they are looking for someone to just listen. By inviting people to come and share, they sometimes come to discover their own gifts and, given the resources, they begin to help themselves and to reach out into the community. As we go out to the people in their homes and apartments, we come in contact with individuals of all ages who are struggling because they lack some resource to help themselves. For those who may need extended help, we have a Catholic social service worker available.

WORKSHOPS AT GENERAL MOTORS

General Motors International Headquarters is on the edge of St. Agnes Parish. Each day 40,000 people drive in from the suburbs to the New Center area, where we are the most immediate parish. An outreach program is offered each fall and spring, where concerns are shared and topics ranging from "Gospel and Secular Life" to "Culture and Poverty" are discussed.

MINISTRY TO THE ARCHDIOCESE

The people of St. Agnes parish intend to survive, to make an impact on the diocese, and to make a significant contribution to making Detroit the first renaissance city in the nation. St. Agnes intends to be a revolutionary parish according to the model of Paul:

> "Your heart and mind must be renewed by a spiritual revolution so that you can put on the new self that has been created in God's way in the goodness and holiness of the Truth" (Ephesians 4:24).

St. Agnes is Catholic in the fullest and deepest sense—inter-racial, inter-class, inter-community. We are a church of the poor and the affluent, of the aged and the young, of the handicapped and the gifted. Where there is fear of people different from ourselves, we bring friendship; where there is embarrassment with the poor, we offer understanding; where there is crime and violence, we create an environment of reconciliation. St. Agnes believes in the new spirituality of the parish and of the people. The heart and soul of parish spirituality and St. Agnes is Eucharist and contemplative prayer that leads to action for justice and Christian service. We believe that every person has a special grace and ministry, not only for oneself and one's family, but for one's city and the world. "You may be different from me, but we were born involved in each other."

NEW BEGINNING EXPERIENCE

1980 was the year of the Family. Each Sunday a family was

featured in the parish bulletin as the family for the week. They read the Scripture, led the offertory procession and carried the parish candle to their home for a week. But many said they had no story to tell, that they were nobodies. The poorest of the poor are those who are poor in their own eyes! Before one can believe in God, one has to believe in oneself. Something was needed for the many who did not believe in, have hope for or love themselves. A parish team member chanced upon the New Beginning Experience. Within a year twenty-five percent of the parish had gone through the program. Although originally designed for divorced and separated Catholics, New Beginning Experience has proved to be a great benefit to the widowed, single, divorced and married individuals of all faiths as well. Each weekend, which is designed to be a time of closure of the past and a new beginning of the present, helps people deal with the psychological grief process that is connected with many events in life and offers an opportunity for turning the pain into an adventure of grace. A trained team leads participants through the quiet, reflective and spiritual program, which is also non-threatening and simple.

These distinctive programs that emerged at St. Agnes still seemed to be too much for many of the people. Strong resistance to meet in one another's homes persisted because so many had already been "ripped off" and every stranger was a potential threat. Fear and mistrust remained deep-seated in the neighborhoods. Yet a movement had begun, a new consciousness was developing, fresh energy was being generated. We were not yet disciples, but we were no longer strangers. We were ready to take the next steps on that immense journey of becoming disciples and apostles of Jesus.

What we needed was a common radical spiritual experience that would break through the walls of insulation and isolation that had made us a "lonely crowd" and discover the "hidden mystery" at work in us that made us the body of Christ. The instrument for this was a Parish Renewal Weekend during the 1981 Lenten Formation Program.

This program is basically a reconciliation and healing retreat that the pastoral team initiates with the people; the people then "turn the table" on the pastoral team giving them a retreat in turn as a way of restoring the pastor and pastoral team to spiritual leadership with the people and for the people.

The process of the retreat allows people to come into touch with their very personal life experience of the Church through penetrating questions that are responded to in writing and shared with others. Everyone recognizes his or her need to be forgiven, but few recognize their power to forgive and to heal each other. In one of the groups, I heard a woman reach out to the woman across from her and say, "I have seen you every Sunday for the past eighteen years, but have never spoken to you. Will you forgive me for not talking to you?" Everyone began to share their faith stories and the story of their wounds and hurts—sometimes going back forty years or more! The retreats were incredible experiences of bonding and creating memories. Healing and reconciliation happened again and again in chain-reaction. A new vision of what church could be was being experienced as new communities emerged from common spiritual explorations.

Especially helpful was the growing clarification and distinctions between parish organizations, ministry groups, growth groups and small Christian communities. "There are a variety of gifts and a variety of ministries." How long it has taken us to recognize the stages and developments in our own parish family, to know that not everyone has to do everything at the same time and the same way! Most have an experience and sense of being a "Church," a pilgrim church on a journey, moving from the "multitude" model to the models of small communities of disciples and ministers.

At a seminar retreat of "Spirituality and Reaching Out into Justice and Peace" in August of 1981, twenty-five participants prayed over and reflected upon the themes: Black Christian Values, Building Community, Risk and Reaching Out, Social Justice and Peace. We began where we were, looking at the *mirror* of our own lives—family tensions, sickness, unemployment, violence in the neighborhood. Then we looked through the *window* of our lives to the wider needs and problems in the parish, Detroit, the country and the world. We wrestled with the questions of relating world problems of racism, poverty, arms race, federal cutbacks to the small groups we already have in the parish. Questions like, "Why can't I see my neighborhood poverty connected to the multi-national corporations?" or "Is it a healing or wounding thing to relate my personal family problems to the world situation?" Retreat participants saw the need for "intermediate windows" that could link local windows in St. Agnes Parish with world windows.

During the summer of 1982, Jean Vanier gave the Faith and Sharing Retreat at Sacred Heart Seminary and more than twenty of the parishioners attended this retreat. From this, a woman's prayer fraternity began and continues to meet each month.

In September of 1983, PRH, "Personality and Human Relations" sessions began at St. Agnes and it has become the regional center for the mid-western states. PRH deals with the human being in the process of personal growth. It is the development, deployment, the liberation and the healing of the adult personality. What happens to people of any faith or of no faith is that the transcendent dimension of their own being comes alive for them. Christians, in conjunction with this, often begin to experience God within themselves in coming in touch with their own inner reality. This international program is an educational process in self-growth that enables an individual to experience his or her inner being or contemplative core.

In 1984-1985 in response to invitations to give parish retreats, a parish retreat team was developed and continues to offer several retreats in the area each year.

The Rosa Parks Family Educational Center opened in the basement of St. Agnes Church in March of 1985 with nineteen pre-school children and one superb, dedicated teacher. Due to lack of funds, many more children had to be turned away. Seventeen of these children have single parents who can afford only $10 per month (if that!), which does not even cover the cost of supplies.

As an integral part of the project, the parent(s) are required to attend four parallel programs designed to improve the quality of family/community life: counseling, parenting, practical courses (i.e., budgeting, hygiene) and the practice of domestic arts. Through these dual programs, which focus on the educational, psychological-social, moral and physical aspects of living, the hope is to form and re-form well-rounded, responsible and successful citizens who can come closer to realizing their full human potential.

In March of 1984, exploration began with a dream for an Ecumenical Contemplative Center at St. Agnes Church. Established bonds with the Episcopal Church of the Messiah deepened. Our journey over the years, the people who inspired us along the way and the continuous Emmaus experience of our hearts burning within us as He talked to us along the way made us bold. And, we were compelled in January of 1986 to announce and prophesy over ourselves that we are a contemplative community—invited and drawn by His love "to live in God's heart at the heart of the city, because it is His dwelling place ... in the very heart of the city of God."

We consciously covenant ourselves with the *Fraternities of Jerusalem*. Founded in Paris in the 1970's, they include solitaries, family group members and lay fraternities. We identify with their rule that states, in part, that "Christ carried on an unceasing struggle with the world's outrages and yet with an ever-deepening incarnation in the heart of everyday reality ... to be in the world means just that: to reveal and find God at its heart, in renewed awareness of its primal beauty and in joyful anticipation of its happiness to come."

We resonate with the spirituality of Charles de Foucauld, the *Little Brother of Jesus*, who spent four years in our parish. We continue to be inspired by the "free to be nothing" spirituality of *Mother Teresa* and her sisters, who lived two years with us. We work at the Hospitality, Corporal and Spiritual centers of Dorothy Day and the *Catholic Worker Movement*.

We are challenged by the *communities of Jean Vanier* to recognize our own handicaps and to allow our woundedness to open us more freely, more fully to others in their brokenness. We are affiliated with the *Community of Transfiguration* near Edinburgh, with *Focus Point* in Dublin and with the *Little Brothers and Sisters of the Eucharist* in Cleveland.

We remember that Jesus was a city person. He prayed over the city; He loved the city; He wept over the city; He worked in it. He loved the city crowds. He walked often through the city and knew it well. He celebrated the first Eucharist in the city and it was there that Jesus initiated his community, the Church. Jesus died at the gate of the city. There, He rose from the dead. His final words to his disciples were, "Stay in the city, then, until you are clothed with the power from on high " (Luke 24:49).

Jesus' love of the city and his compassion and concern for the multitudes, for the "little ones," is an imperative for a Contemplative Prayer Community in the heart of the city. Jesus is deep in the heart of this metropolitan city of four and a half million people. West Grand Boulevard is a contemporary Via Dolorosa, a Way of the Cross, that so many are compelled to tread each day. Rosa Parks Boulevard is a renaissance neighborhood—a light, hope and promise of today, of tomorrow.

This contemplative community is anchored in a parish of ordinary and faithful people who have chosen to continue to live in the heart of the city. Through their own experience of the hardships of city life with its alienations, its struggles, its works, its restraints, its anonymity and violence, they know the stress, the noise and pollution, the joys and sorrows, the evil and the goodness of the city.

They live in solidarity with the people of the city and wish to offer them some kind of Nazareth or Bethany or Emmaus freely open to all; to offer them a place of deep silence alive with prayer, a place of rest and healing, a home where all people, whatever their social or religious background, age or outlook on life, are invited to come and to share in a common search for contemplation in Christ.

The experts tell us it takes five to ten years to form small Christian communities. We believe that we are well on the journey and there is no turning back. He has called; we are following! Perhaps a short section from Morris West's *The Clowns of God* says it for everyone:

> "You should know that you are not here by your own design. You were led here, step by step, on different roads, through many apparent accidents; but, always, it was the finger of God that beckoned you.

You are not the only community thus brought together. There are many others, all over the world: in the forests of Russia, in the jungles of Brazil, in places you would never dream. They are all different; because men's needs and habits are different. Yet they are all the same; because they have followed the same beckoning finger, and bound themselves by the same love. They did not do this of themselves. They could not, just as you could not, without a special prompting of grace.

You were prompted for a reason. Even as I speak, the adversary begins to stalk the earth, roaring destruction! So, in evil times which are now upon us, you are chosen to keep the small flame of love alight, to nurture the seeds of goodness in this small place, until the day when the Spirit sends you out to light other candles in a dark land and plant new seeds in a blackened earth.

I am with you now; but tomorrow I shall be gone. You will be alone and afraid. But I leave my peace with you and my love. And you will love one another as I have loved you.

Please! He urged them to cheerfulness. You must not be sad! The gift of the Holy Spirit is gladness of heart."

2

Free for Conversion

Each of us has a bottomless heart. Each of us is a field in which an immense treasure is sown. Each of us consciously and unconsciously wait upon that mystery. Have I begun my conversion? my spiritual revolution? I am uncomfortable with those "i-o-n" words. They suggest a state of accomplishment or completeness. I believe the Christian experience is always the beginning of something—something ongoing, never completed, very much a journeying and pilgriming. Is conversion ever completed? I think it a most dangerous temptation to believe that I have converted. The great temptation before Vatican II was to believe that we totally possessed the truth. That faith in Jesus was a reality behind us, already accomplished, rather than that our faith is something ahead of us, yet to be completed, and that Jesus is ahead of us—that we have not caught up to Him, that He is still the one we are searching for, something we are trying to discover.

Arrogance dies slowly; we had an incredible arrogance before Vatican II. Thanks to the change that continues, we are discovering the most important virtue of the New Testament— a certain humbleness to know that we have been wrong, to know that we have sinned, and we continue to sin. One of the Fathers of the Church a long time ago spoke about the holy lie, the sacred lie, and all of us are victims of the holy lie, the sacred lie that we tell to ourselves. The pharisees are too often our closest identity. The sin of the pharisees is worth meditating upon. They thought that they were holy. They thought that they had the truth. They thought that they were different. They thought that they could judge others. And unconsciously, all of us are pharisees. Is there not a little of that in each of us? And so it is with a certain amount of uneasiness that I reflect upon conversion and ask myself the question, "Have I converted?"

How dangerous it is to be a born Catholic, because we grow up with the illusion that we have all truth, that we have already arrived, that we have caught up with Jesus. Yet Jesus is always going on ahead of us, always waiting for us. The way of Jesus is the way of pilgrimage. There is no way to pilgrimage to Jesus except through a continuing converting, a constant turning to Jesus. It is not easy to follow Jesus. In fact, He reverses the situation. If it ever depended upon us to follow Jesus, we would have long lost that path, given up the journey. The mystery is that Jesus is always following us. In a paradoxical way, He is more our disciple than we are His. That is the infinite patience of Jesus, trying to help us to come to understand that He really loves us. I suggest the following questions. When you think of converting, to whom are you converting? From what are you converting? The questions of Jesus are always questions that demand change. That demand a turning, a turning away from ourselves, from this world identification, our so-called accomplishments, from our achievements, that we might see how poor we are, and how infinite the distance that lies ahead of us. Jesus comes in so many different ways, but each of us has our own way of flight and escape from Jesus, our avoidance of Him. This is why the beginning of the year, or Lent or Advent can be a time of anguish, and yet, at the same moment, a time of joy, because something is stirred within us. Now is the great beginning; anything is possible. For a while, we listen very carefully. The catalyst of scriptural readings is so important. When we think of conversion, of converting, to whom do you turn? It is one thing to turn to God, but it is important to be honest with that God we turn to. Whose God? What of the God that we carry within us? When you pray, to whom do you pray? Do you pray to the Father? Do you pray to the Son: Do you pray to the Holy Spirit? Or, do you pray to "To whom it may concern"? Who is it to whom we pray? What part of me is turning to Jesus: What part of me is His? It is one thing to have the thoughts of a Christian community in my mind. It is another to turn with our hearts in moments of fervor. In his letter to the Ephesians, Paul said,

> "You must give up your old way of life. You must put aside your old self which gets corrupted by following illusory desires. Your mind must be moved by *a spiritual revolution* so that you can put on the new self that has been created in God's way in the goodness and holiness of the truth." (Eph 4:22-24)

There are all kinds of prayer and all kinds of theologies that we can turn to of ourselves. There is a kind of conversion that is totally beyond us, impossible by ourselves. Again and again, in the most decisive moments of Jesus' preaching, His disciples turned to Him and complained that what He was asking was impossible, and Jesus never backed away from what He said. There is a kind of prayer that is utterly impossible without Jesus. There are all kinds of prayer that we can do just out of the human condition—all kinds of prayer arising out of human creativity, human friendship. But there is a kind of prayer that only Jesus can do. There are all kinds of work that we can do out of our human talent, our background. But there is a kind of ministry that only Jesus can do. Each one of us intuitively knows that we go so far with Him, and then we hit or push some kind of "hold" button and remain there. There is a holding pattern in each of our lives. Each of us can go so far and no further. Each of us has an implicit contract. We never recognize it until we are called to move beyond that point. And then somehow, that refrain from the gospel, the sixth chapter of John, "and many of His disciples no longer walked with Him." The partial conversion—so easy to take those first few steps; but to move beyond, how difficult!

How much more converted I seemed years ago. How easy was the conversion before Vatican II. How easy to know what was right and what was wrong. How easy when we could just put ourselves under the normal umbrella with minimal requirement. How easy when we really do not know. How uncomfortable when we are asked to go further. There is a familiar reading from Mark's gospel that I find more disturbing this year than ever before—there were many who were reluctant to follow Jesus. Luke describes Jesus' going out into the desert as being led by the spirit, and Mark in his usual style is much more concrete. He said that Jesus was *driven* out into the desert—with reluctance, hesitancy and resistance. Jesus knew what He was getting into, that He really faced the devil. Throughout Mark's gospel there is a Jesus that knows all too well the direction He is going toward. His prayer is not answered by His Father. He asked that if it be possible that He would not have to complete that mission. He received no answer. Our Lord was not very successful as an evangelist. When I first began to reflect on evangelization, I thought it would be very exciting until I realized that Jesus was not successful as an evangelist—in His preaching, in His miracles, and most obviously, in His disciples. The ultimate work of Jesus' evangelization, His ultimate act of evangelization was His suffering, and His death. Evangelization is rooted in that—not in programming, not in muscular Christianity, not in media, but an incredible obedience, a listening and faithfulness to the call of His Father.

In Mark's gospel a volunteer, a young man runs up to Jesus, and falling on his knees asks Jesus a second question. "What more can I do?" Be very careful of the *second* question. The response to the first question is always simple. The young man asked, "What must I do to inherit eternal life?" And Jesus gave him a straight answer, but the young man wanted to go further. He said I've kept all these from my earliest days. What more? And then Jesus looked steadily at him and loved him, and because he loved him, he gave the second response. "There is one thing you lack. GO and sell everything you own. Give your money to the poor and you will have treasures in heaven, and then COME follow me." (Mk 10:17-21)

This is another of Jesus' impossible invitations, one that is least responded to even in our day, total love, unconditional discipleship. What is especially striking is that Jesus said, "Go" and then, "Come." With all of the rest of His disciples He said, "Come." He invited them to be with Him first, and only after that experience did He expect them to go and have an effect upon others, to change them. To this volunteer, this rich young man, Jesus simply said, "Go," and "Come, follow me." He said it in the context that He looked upon Him with love. What an immense moment! Conversion is never one moment. It is a continuing life process.

Perhaps we are not converting because we do not experience the need. We do not experience the need for Jesus. Who is the person who trembles before God? Who of us is facing the living God? Who really puts on ashes? Who prostrates himself before the altar? Who cries in the sanctuary? Liturgy is an awesome time, because the word of God is uttered with new power. Every Mass there is a new sowing. There is new seed "whose power working within us can do infinitely more than we can ask or imagine." What of me belongs to Him? My arms, my ears, my hands, my feet? What have I turned over to Him totally, not partially? Converting is not something I do. Conversion is the radical work of Jesus in me. Conversion only happens to contemplatives. Is there any way of being Christian, except contemplatively? Is there any experience of Jesus except a mystical experience? God is speaking now. He is always speaking. His word never ceases to vibrate in every fiber of us. The Good News is to dare to believe that He is already in us; conversion comes from the inside out. There is a depth of His presence in each of us that can only be experienced in prayer—not a prayer of words, not even a prayer of scripture, but lifting and waiting and walking and working for the Lord. The beautiful psalm, Psalm 95 that Christian communities pray every day, says it:

"Harden not your heart this day,
if you hear His voice."

Trying to draw upon that immense treasure that is hidden in each of us, "I will put a new spirit in you." I will give you a new fountain. He is always enjoying us. He is always looking at us with love. Christian contemplation dares to admit to the possibility that Jesus is contemplating me at every moment. That He knows me and loves me. Recall that marvelous passage toward the end of the first chapter of John's gospel, the call of Nathanael. Only in John's gospel do we discover that Jesus did not call His apostles, His twelve randomly one by one, but that His followers were involved in calling each other. Andrew went and found his brother Peter. Have you ever found your brother? Have you ever found your sister? Have you turned them to Jesus? Have you ever brought anyone to Jesus? Can we ever come just by ourselves? Can we only turn ourselves? Now after Jesus called Philip, Philip found Nathanael and said to him,

> "We have found the one Moses wrote about in the law. The one about whom the prophets wrote. He is Jesus, son of Joseph of Nazareth." (Jn 1:45)

"From Nazareth," said Nathanael. "Can anything good come from that place?" "Come and see," replied Philip. Now when Jesus saw Nathanael coming, He said of him, "There is an Israelite who deserves the name incapable of deceit." This is a compliment that was given to no other disciple. Here was a man incapable of deceit. What an extraordinary person Nathanael must have been, to draw from Jesus such a tribute. Only John the Baptist received a greater tribute. Then we wonder why Nathanael did not become the one who was to be a spokesman of the others. The Lord is not compelled to use the best. And we never hear of Nathanael again. He accepted this compliment from Jesus and asked Jesus a question, a profound question. He dared to ask Jesus, "How do you know me?"

Imagine asking Jesus that question. Ask Jesus how does He know you. Nathanael asked that question and Jesus responded, "Before Philip came to call you, I saw you under the fig tree." And Nathanael in utter astonishment cried out, "Rabbi, you are the Son of God. You are the King of Israel." How long before Philip ever found Nathanael, Jesus had found Nathanael! Yes, Jesus finds each of us. Scriptural interpreters, who often have no comment on some of the passages that we are most concerned about, like "I saw you under the fig tree," suggest that Jesus caught Nathanael at prayer, longing and desiring the Messiah, the One who was promised to come.

Jesus is always looking at us. And our prayer, our contemplation is to catch Jesus contemplating us, giving us the immense gift of Himself. Only Jesus could ever change us, convert us, transubstantiate us. How do you know me? What would our conversion experience be? How will you know that you are changing? How will you know when it happens? Is it something past; is it something ongoing; or, is it yet ahead of each of us? Jesus is always moving and so the call is also a matter of following, and walking, running. Paul uses that, to run, to run the race. No practices, no virtues will change us of themselves alone.

A Christian is someone who discovers a mystery in his or her life. He discovers a truth that he knows is revelation, and he is compelled to proclaim it—to share it with others. That is what a prophet is, too. Someone who discovers a meaning, a presence in his or her life, so exciting that they recognize in their life a revelation. Each one of us is a word of God that He hasn't finished uttering, drawing us into that mystery of His image. I have always been impressed with Gandhi, who as an adult never looked in a mirror. The only way he knew of himself was what he found reflected in another. How long could you go without looking in a mirror? Yet, it is good to use even the simple act of looking in a mirror to ask ourselves some of those questions. How do you know me? To know that the deepest experience I will ever have of God is the experience of my own life.

The Eucharist is a call to me to be sacrament. Vatican II dared to describe the church, to describe us, as a sacrament of salvation for the whole world—a sacrament of liberation, a sacrament of transparency. A sacrament is something hidden, yet makes itself felt. There are the sacraments that can only be touched by faith. We are called to be a sacrament that the whole world can see, even though it does not believe, because we are to be that sacrament. Converting to the person of Jesus, converting to the mystery of Eucharist—the sacrament of conversion is Eucharist. The mystery of Jesus converting, changing the reality of us into His presence.

The Eucharist is the invitation to dare to believe that prayer of Paul to him whose power working in us can do infinitely more than we can ask or imagine. Together we believe that the mystery of Eucharist is intended to be a mirror for what he is doing to us, that we are being changed, that there is a spiritual revolution going on in us out of the cumulative presence of His word, of His sacrament, of His people in us. It is easy to be converted to the unknown God because He is a reality that cannot be avoided or evaded. Being converted to Jesus demands new life.

We turn to Jesus when we turn to the mystery of His cross, and of His love. What is difficult is the turn that He does in us. The more we surrender, the more we listen and hear Him. The Lord returns us to the other members of His body. Jesus is good company, but those that He identifies with are not easy company. The sign that we have of turning, of converting to Jesus is that we have new eyes, new ears, new heart and new hands and feet that minister to the only Jesus that we can ever experience directly. The ministry of Jesus in the oppressed, in the poor, in the people that we are least comfortable with. Jesus always calls us to the impossible. He says that very pointedly. "Where I am I want you to be." Something new happens, when we let Jesus contemplate us, when we dare to move beyond the sacred lie, the holy lie, the illusion that we are Jesus, the illusion that we love, the illusion that we believe. The first moment of conversion for the man who went up to prayer, was to lower his head and cry out,

"Lord, be merciful to me, a sinner." (Lk 18:13)

The conversion to humility is not easy, because prayer can be used so easily as an avoidance of God. The call to pray.

There is a new you coming. Go into your room, shut the door and pray to your Father who is in that place and He will hear you. There is a new you coming. You fast, and you open yourself to the things that prevent you from seeing Jesus. Be yourself, because there is no possible turning away from oneself unless we turn to something more. There is a hunger in each of us. We are starved for Jesus, and we shall never experience Him unless we let go of the things that make us unfree. There is a new you coming—when you give yourself to Him. When the disciples came to Jesus and told Him to send the people away, Jesus said, "Give them something to eat. Yourselves." He is still saying that. Every time we celebrate Eucharist, it impels us with His light so that we might feed others. And the Eucharist remains incomplete when we do not go and give of ourselves to those who are most in need of His presence. All of our members need that healing; we need that healing. Yet, only you, only I, can make the choice to offer ourselves freely to Him so that He can break us open, turn us around and knead us into bread for others to eat. There is no point in being Christian, if you do not know that Life will break your heart!

3

Free to be a Disciple

"Make disciples of all people" (Mt 28:19). This is Jesus' final command to his followers. What goes into the making of a disciple? Is Jesus still inviting us "to come and follow?" Disciple is a Christian title that seems to be disappearing because it carries too heavy a burden; yet, it appears 250 times in the New Testament. What enables a person to move from the multitude, the anonymous crowd, to become a follower, a witness of the Gospel, a disciple? Are there steps and stages, passages and transitions? Are there a thousand and one paths that lead to becoming a "friend" of Jesus? Becoming a disciple is a journey, a journey that began before we were born.

> "Before the world was made the Father chose us, chose us in Christ, to be holy and spotless, and to live through love in his presence, determining that we should be his adopted sons and daughters, through Jesus Christ." (Eph 1:4)

"Before we were born we were involved in each other, in Him" and all of life is an unfolding, an unveiling, a re-veal-ation of "this infinite treasure of Christ, kept hidden in God through all the ages."

There is a hunger in each of us that, like the wind, we know not from whence it comes. There is an ever expanding capacity in each person for "more." There is a restless drive and thrust toward the something or someone more than ourselves. We find we are in an energy field, a time-space continuum, that haunts us more and more.

Perhaps the first step of a disciple is discovering that the ultimate loneliness is a loneliness for one's own hidden self, one's mysterious capacity and need for God. This grace and intuition readies one to listen and search. Curiosity draws one along with the multitude until a simple Word, the two-edged sword of the Spirit, a question, an imperative, or someone calling one by name—and then, the blind see and the deaf hear and the crippled walk and the dead arise. One falls to his knees and cries out, "O God, be merciful to me, a sinner," and rises in the awesome freedom of a son or a daughter of God.

Only Jesus makes disciples! I do not discover Him but He is always discovering me, drawing me into a new understanding of myself, of Himself. He can use curiosity like that of Zaccheus "who was anxious to catch a glimpse of Jesus." He fascinates us with an invitation like the rich young man "whom he looked upon with love." He meets us with our problems and our woundedness. We may feel like strangers, but He reveals Himself as our hidden neighbor, friend, sister, brother.

Perhaps the most embarrassing moment for the beginning disciple is when Jesus' goodness and love compels us to face our own unrecognized sin and we are compelled to cry out like Peter, "O Lord, go away from me. I am a sinner" (Lk 5:4). If we truly meet God in our prayer, we would not even dare to lift our head and we would be crying out, "O Lord, be merciful to me, a sinner." The first grace of conversion is to know the truth of oneself, for all truth is holy even though it be truth of one's sin. "If we say that we have no sin, we are liars and there is no truth in us." The best of us is a forgiven sinner. The disciple must be honest with God and honest with him or her self. The grace of recognizing one's identity as a sinner brings the grace of freedom to change and grow, the *need* to follow Jesus is deeply liberating.

The call to be a disciple is universal. Everyone is called under the last imperative of Jesus:

"Go make disciples of all people." (Mt 28:19)
"For He is the true light that enlightens every person who comes into the world." (Jn 1:9)

The call is given, the seed is sown, but the response might take most of a lifetime. There is only one sadness in life, only one possible failure—that is "not to be a saint," not to be a disciple, not to have discovered the way, the truth and the life. Everyone is on the same journey, everyone is filled with the same hunger, everyone consciously or unconsciously is a pilgrim of the absolute. What stories will be told throughout all eternity of the Hounds of God, the "pilgrims of the absolute!" Most of the stories will not be about us finding God, but of Him finding us. We are always letting go of Him. He is always breaking into our lives, finding us. What a gospel each of us could write on the ways of God touching our lives and drawing us to Himself—or, the ways we have *escaped* from God. Every person's life is the story of running to or away from God. Who does not recognize Psalm 139 as one's own story?

> "Where can I go from your presence? If I go up to the heavens, you are there. If I sink to the nether world you are present there. If I take the wings of the dawn and settle at the farthest limits of the sea, even there your hand shall guide me and your right hand hold me fast. If I say surely the darkness shall hide me and light shall be my night, even the darkness is not dark to you, the night is as bright as the day; for darkness is as light with you."

There is never a moment of our lives that we are not in "danger of God," in danger of being "seduced" by God. Even Oscar Wilde was compelled to admit that "at least once in his life each person walks with Christ to Emmaus."

Each must face the cost of discipleship. What do I have to lose? I may lose my "identity"—my "cover," my masks, my illusions—Jesus seduces us only so far and then we must choose ever more decisively and radically. At times Jesus seems to be a tempter, an enemy, and "many of his disciples no longer walk with Him." The multitudes thin out, the followers straggle after. The disciples are confronted, "Will you go away?" Disciples so easily become strangers to Jesus. Jesus keeps on moving ("He went on ahead" Lk 19:28), and if we do not keep pace with Him, we may all too soon hear His judgment, "I do not know you" (Mt 25:13).

In the New Testament, the vocation to special discipleship is portrayed as a vocation to hardships too severe to be generally accepted. Generosity is more than demanded by a master whose own vocation came to its ultimate expression in suffering.

The journey into discipleship is unique for each person. While I was directing a seminar on "Spiritualities of Contemporary Lay Movements," one of the young leaders of the Marriage Encounter program shared that the most significant impact of Vatican II on him was that he felt he was "free to discover his own God." I have not been able to forget his words. What an incredible experience it must be to discover one's own God, to find one's own prayer, to enter those terrible and mysterious depths out of which one cries "I believe!" I *know* Him in whom I believe! This is what the older books call a "mystical experience." No wonder it is being said that the "Christians of the future would be mystics or they would not be." I am not speaking of "Strange Encounters of the Third Kind" or of rare and exotic psychic phenomena, rather of an authentic experience of God in the midst of everyday life which can be known very deeply, even if it is incapable of being analyzed and put into words. I am not talking about Trappist monks and Carmelite contemplatives, or even about priests and sisters, but about "ordinary people," grassroots people, who are called the "faithful" without them knowing the depth of that unconscious compliment.

The special grace of our times is that more and more Christians are experiencing a new understanding of their identity and call. Fewer are content to be passive members on Sunday. It is no longer enough to be anonymous members of a parish. Many are experiencing a need to be visible disciples of Jesus. But where does this prophecy, this vision, this expectation, hope or dream come from? How does this conversion happen? Sometimes it is meeting with searching people; many times it is reading a book, listening to a sermon, seeing a movie like "Gandhi." Everyone has a gift and a talent. "You are not your own." "Come and follow Me." Something buried in us for half a life time suddenly comes to the surface and we can no longer suppress it.

In the past, specially gifted people seemed to be called to be disciples. Now Jesus seems to be calling very ordinary people, people who do not see themselves as anyone special, who feel that they know little and have nothing to share with others. But these are the very people that Jesus always calls. We become special when we begin to follow Jesus and allow Him to live more consciously in our lives. In surprising and simple ways, He is always speaking to us. He is at the heart of the world and at the heart of each of us, especially at the fragile center where we are afraid—of ourselves, of others.

Every crisis holds a hidden grace. The crisis of vocations and ordained ministry has touched off an evolution and re-discovery of ministry and discipleship. Church vocations are no longer seen as only for the young and single, full time and life long, but for people at every stage of their life—full time, part time and short time as well as long term. Some have created their own ministries.

Necessity and crisis is the mother of new perceptions and insights. Everything changes, nothing is finalized in politics or economics, in love or in faith. Every person is in process, coming or going, in development, in transformation.

Some growth and development is so slow as to be almost imperceptible, like that of mountains which are measured in centuries by inches or like the dawning of a great truth in the hearts of a people. How long will it take for the Gospel to penetrate every strata and level of culture and society? Is anyone waiting in the shopping mall to be called?

"The Holy Spirit broods over our world with ah! bright wings." The new depth of personal faith and prayer is one of the great spiritual "fallouts" of Vatican II. Sad to say, or perhaps wonderful to report, every generation spiritually has to reinvent the wheel, rediscover fire. Because every generation attempts to settle down and forget the journey, the fire dies and is not passed on to the children. Why must we wait for twenty years after nuclear bombs are dropped on population centers of Japan for Vatican II to begin to awaken the Christian world?

The present situation requires and demands, much more radically than before, the personal involvement of each one in his decision for faith. Karl Rahner considers that the most striking characteristics of the spirituality of the parish today is the dialectical unity of the *solitude of the faith* and the *fraternal community of faith*. It is no longer enough to believe what almost everybody else believed and was born into. Today, the Christian faith must be lived, always anew, in a secularized world in a context of atheism and technology. It is only at a level of radical, solitary religious experience that the Christian can begin to live his and her faith today.

The Holy Spirit breathes upon the earth and fiery seeds enkindle the once nameless and faceless anonymous crowd. Once people begin to discover their own God, and their "hidden self begins to grow strong," the ripples of their Spirit radiate to others. By an intuition of the Spirit and a kinship of grace they are drawn to others of the same Spirit, "whose power working in them, can do infinitely more than they could ask or imagine" (Eph 3:20).

Out of the individual experience, solitude of faith converges on the fraternal community of faith, one creating the capacity for the other and deepening the original experience. Could the ancient Pentecost experience have been more than an external phenomenon of mighty wind and tongues of fire coming from the outside? Could it have been an eruption from within, through the interaction of the hidden Spirit in each of those gathered together?

Synergy is a relatively new English word, meaning an interaction of energies that bring about a new quality of energy. The term has taken on psychological significance, but perhaps its deepest relevance is in the realm of the Spirit. Here the coming together of different graces or charisms opens up manifestations of community long hidden and now being brought forth to meet the needs of our day.

One of the more significant evolutions of the 20th century is the phenomenon of the *single person* and the new freedom available to each individual person. The secular city has guaranteed anonymity and autonomy. As never before individuals have been freed from the negative pressure and power

of family, neighborhood, and society. Only for rare individuals has such freedom existed in the past. " . . . and (they)
withdrew into themselves and began to secrete a protective
shell because they thought that they were alone and no one
cared."(Evely. *That Man Is You*) How is a person drawn out
of his or her "protective shell?" Aloneness and anonymity,
namelessness and without friends are descriptions of too many
people of our day. And so it was in the time of Jesus. The
great gift Jesus offers to people is that someone cares, someone
is there for them, that no one ever need be alone again. Jesus is
the great teacher of friendship, the facilitator of bringing
people together. Jesus is the great welcomer, the party-giver,
the gatherer of people, introducing people to one another so
that they can come to know and love each other. Imagine all
the people who have come to know one another through their
mutual contact with Jesus. The deepest friendships come
because of a mutual friendship with Jesus. Jesus enjoys his
friends most when they come to know and enjoy, appreciate
and love one another. Jesus loves the multitudes, yet He seems
to love even more the small groups of disciples. The multitude
do not know one another; the disciples come to know one
another. The disciples learn to talk to one another and to
share more and more with each other. The disciples become a
family of friends.

Jesus is the master friend-maker. And so his disciples are
friend-makers. Jesus was always reaching out to meet people,
to begin a friendship. He talked to everyone, sinner or saint,
politician or tax collector, lawyer or soldier, woman or child.
He loved to be invited for dinner and often invited himself! He
introduced his friends to one another. How good it is to be a
friend of the friends of Jesus!

Someone has said that Jesus never went to the temple to
pray. He went there to meet people. How he enjoyed them!
Wherever people were, Jesus went there. He didn't wait like
John the Baptist at the banks of the River Jordan. He
immersed himself in their lives. He observed them closely and
listened to them deeply. He listened to them so deeply that
many of them told him more than they had ever intended. He
loved them. He accepted them where they were and for whom

they wanted to become. There was nothing negative in Him to touch off the negative in themselves. They experienced their hidden goodness in His presence. He was always "hatching" them by His warmth and affirmation. They experienced His current of warm affection and wanted to come out of their "protective shells" where "they thought they were alone and no one cared."

Every person is wounded by one's family or by society. Each of us is in need of healing. Each person has an infinite capacity for growth and that growth will resume its rightful course as soon as it is given an opportunity and the adequate environment is created. Every child is completely dependent; left to oneself, he or she is psychologically incapable of coping with life. Children need to be accepted and protected by someone else. Not until then will they feel safe and be able to deal with life. The child must feel that someone is so concerned with her that she has been drawn into the safety of the orbit of their life. Only then is the vacuum of the child's dependency filled, only then is he in a condition in which natural growth and development can take place.

Most of us receive enough in our families to *survive*; few have received enough to move into and unto maximum growth capacity. No one can do it alone. Nor can anyone do it with only one other significant person. No one can ever understand himself as he is worth being understood. No one can love herself as she is worth being loved. Each of us has a capacity for thirty, sixty, one hundred friends in our lives. Yet how rarely that ever happens. How sad that we discover so little of our hidden selves.

We are invited into an ever expanding community of friendship, a family or families of friends. This is the great spiritual journey of what we call "Church." Jesus gathered people together, all kinds of people, and told them a great secret—a secret hidden from all previous generations. He helped them to see that they were sisters and brothers, that they were family and belong to one another. This is the Good News! The Kingdom is already here because Jesus is here with us and in us. He identifies Himself with and pours his Spirit into every person. "He enlightens everyone who comes into the world."

We are the family of God, a kingdom which cannot be seen, yet is already here.

If one listens with faith to the Gospel long enough, it will begin to speak in new ways to the heart. "Ask and you shall receive, seek and you will find, knock and it shall be opened to you." For most of my life, I heard this passage as saying the same thing three times over. Now I hear it as a progression—if I ask, I shall receive something, enough to keep me seeking. When I continue to seek, I will discover something that will confirm my journey, enough to knock on someone's door or dial someone's number. When I have knocked on a few doors or phoned a few people, I always have found someone who also has been drawn into the same process and a new little community begins.

The tide goes out only to come in again. The shore line is always changing, expanding, receding. The disciples are most disciples when they are at sea, about to drown, when they are praying out of fear, when they are without security, recognition, effectiveness. Disciples are happy to let Jesus fall asleep, and be busy about many things. Storms and oppression compel them to awaken the sleeping Christ with them or within them. Faith does not stay at high tide; it ebbs away and fatalism so easily takes its place. The leap of faith so easily becomes a limp and the exuberance becomes a lament. How hard it is to believe that Jesus "goes on working!"

Disciples are made by other disciples. Where does one find a disciple today? Someone who lives the Gospel? Someone who creates in you the desire and possibility of making the Gospel come alive? Someone who activates that hidden self within? To be open, to be attentive, to listen, to ask questions are such special graces in themselves. There are stepping stones, there are footprints in the sands, there are certain symptoms of those who dare to dream dreams and are ready to pay the price to make them become a reality.

When I was in high school, I heard about the "Catholic Worker Movement." I was curious and eventually met Lou and Justine Murphy, the founders of the Detroit Catholic Worker Movement in 1937. Having started the St. Francis House of Hospitality, where hundreds of men were fed in their bread line each day, their home was open to any stranger or homeless person. In this unique Christian environment, they raised their seven children. As a young seminarian, when I visited them or worked in the bread line, they taught me that those in need are the "ambassadors of Christ," that personal responsibility and initiative for others and voluntary poverty are clear invitations and challenges of the Gospel. These special disciples of Jesus left an indelible mark upon me. I still wonder how they came to make the decision and to remain so faithful to it. I continue to be moved by the deep and constant call and need to live the Gospel more visibly, by the commitment to continue Jesus' presence to those who have no one else, made by these ordinary lay people—true disciples of Jesus.

The Gospel does not let us forget that the problems of the world and the crises of the city are our problems too. Jesus loves us too much to allow us to remain unconscious oppressors. If we dare to ask Him like Paul, "Who are you?" He will tell us, "I am Jesus whom you are oppressing." Inside every problem there is hidden potential, hidden grace. The Gospel asks us to let go of some of our comfort, energy and time. Our prophets begin to tell us that we cannot be fully American and fully Christian much longer! The call is becoming, has already become for many, an imperative to discover our unique gift, our charism of ministry and community. "To each is given a gift to build up the community." Only Jesus creates this kind of community. Though it already exists, how few recognize and experience it, Him, ourselves. "If you but knew the gift of God and who it is who is speaking to you."

Each of us carries "trace" elements of a great dream. Each bears a hidden prophecy, each carries seeds that are intended to renew the face of the earth. We have become aware of the biological genetic code, yet only dimly do we recognize the spiritual genetic code that the Spirit is always activating. "I have come that you may bear fruit, and bear fruit abundantly."

A disciple is someone who experiences a presence, a joy, a peace within him or herself so deeply that he or she is compelled to share it with others. A hidden mission, priesthood, vocation lives in each of us. As this begins to emerge, we find other people who also know that they have been "haunted" by Jesus, who are drawn to one another that they might grow together in Him.

Perhaps our most hidden sin is that we have so little time for one another. We need so much more than television offers. We need to relearn how to relate eye to eye, hand to hand, heart to heart. We have to encourage one another to keep walking toward Him, toward joy, toward truth. We need one another to simplify our lives and to live where God is most to be found in deeper presence with each other. We need to be purified, to be freed of excess baggage in order to become more joyful, filled with God. Fragile people are such a revelation of God. We need to pray for our world. Our world is really hopeless. Only through Jesus' love can it be saved. What Jesus can do with a little piece of bread, He can do with us!

The Gospel calls for fullness of life through intentional, deliberate, free community. A plurality of interacting people releases immense energy in each person. Diversity of personalities and temperaments, weaknesses and strengths call forth hidden potential in the individuals and in the community.

I have seen this at Lopianno with the Focolare Movement, at Taize with Brother Roger and the monks, and at L'Arch with Jean Vanier. In his summit book, *Community and Growth*, Jean Vanier writes,

> "We all carry our deep wound, which is the wound of our loneliness. We find it hard to be alone, and we try to flee from this in hyperactivity, through television and in a million other ways.
>
> . . . We have to realize that this wound is inherent in the human condition and that what we have to do is walk with it instead of fleeing from it. We cannot accept it until we discover that we are loved by God, just as we are, and that the Holy Spirit in a mysterious way is living at the Centre of the wound."

From Africa comes a new experience of vital participation in a common life—a community that exercises a vital influence on one another, a power of being together, a life-bond of vital current, a unity of life that can be touched and handled. At all ceremonies of any importance—birth, marriage, death—the ancestors preside. Together they participate in a mystic power, essence, reality. Community is experienced as a means of life in which one participates in order to exist. There is an element of cosmic connectedness, a corporate spirit, a "world soul." All the vital energies, all the currents of their ancestors' blood, all the life which God has placed in them to be carried on and made fruitful have burst into being. No wonder some dare to say, "We possess power and life only in community." This interaction of beings on one another, living and dead, visible and invisible, is a love that lets life and spirit flow into one another, giving them light by which to come to see themselves and to enkindle a fire to energize and empower each other. Joy feeds the soul and uplifts the spirit. Faith sustains. Presence heals.

"Where two or three are gathered together in my name, there I am in their midst" is not simply a beautiful Scriptural verse; rather, it is a description of an essential connection for a spiritual reality that cannot exist without His presence and action. If He is not present, then two or three cannot truly be "together." As Henri Nouwen wrote,

> "True solitude, far from being the opposite of community life, is the place where we come to realize that we were together before we came together and that community life is not a creation of human will but an obedient response to the reality of our being united. Many people who have lived together for years and whose love for one another has been tested more than once know that the decisive experience in their life was not that they were able to hold together but that they were held together. That, in fact, we are a community not because we like each other or have a common task or project, but because we are called together by God."

The most startling command Jesus gives to his disciples is "Go, make disciples of all people." He knew that the only way we continue to be disciples is in the effort and struggle to make others disciples. Before Jesus could dare give this command, his disciples had to experience those moments when he drew them to himself and said, as in John 15,

> "All that I have received from the Father, I have made known to you, therefore you are my friends.... As the Father has loved me, so I have loved you.... As the Father has sent me, so I send you."

Then Jesus gave them Himself under the form of Bread and Wine. Eucharist is the sacrament of discipleship; Eucharist creates the community of disciples. Only Jesus with us enables us to "make disciples," to make friends, to make family, to make community.

Jesus is the Word made flesh, the Word renders Him present under the form of Bread and Wine. The Word reveals His hidden presence in the least of his brethren; the prophetic Word of God breathed over bread and wine and breathed into ordinary people transforms them into disciples, releases the hidden energy and power within them and makes them disciples, burning bushes that enkindle the world. To experience discipleship is to experience both *kenosis* and *pleroma*, the emptying of oneself and the filling up again by God. It is to know that the further one walks, the more total the awareness of being an unfaithful person through whom God continues to work.

4

Free for Evangelization

"Now is the favorable time. This is the day of salvation"—
the hour of Evangelization. We are called to be ambassadors
of Christ. We are invited to be His Word to others. The call to
Evangelization is the call to "give others something to eat—
yourselves!" Evangelization is a passionate involvement and
identification with the broken body of Christ which leads to
death and resurrection. "Where I am I want you to be."

The Lord's Prayer is actually the prayer of Evangelization—the prayer of Jesus, which He gives to his evangelizers. The call to prayer is a preamble to evangelization, to
being sent out to make visible the mystery of Christ's presence
with us. Evangelization is a visible manifestation of the reality
of prayer and the work of reconciliation. God reconciled us to
Himself and gave us the work of handing on this reconciliation. God in Christ was "evangelizing" the world to
Himself. He has entrusted to us this work of evangelizing.

To what degree can I believe that I am His ambassador, His
presence, that I hold His power? What does it mean to reconcile, to establish bonds, to establish kinship, to establish friendship, to evangelize? What was in Christ at that moment when
He became fully aware of His mission to evangelize? How free
am I to evangelize?

Evangelization is not one person, one thing. It is everyone,
each in a unique way, each in a different way—sometimes
consciously and consistently, and, other times, not so consciously and consistently—following Christ. Evangelization is

a *community of disciples*, witnesses of Christ—a community which in spite of all of its deficiencies is a community precisely because all of its members form together with Christ Himself, because they bear in their hearts the indelible mark of the Christian.

Luke gave his witness: "I must proclaim the Good News of the kingdom of God to the other cities too; for I was sent for this purpose." Earlier, Jeremiah had proclaimed: "But then it became like fire burning in my heart, imprisoned in my bones. I grew weary holding it in, and I could not endure it." And Paul, after Damascus, lived his whole life knowing, "Woe to me if I do not preach the Gospel."

John wrote to the Christian community of his conviction and his experience of being called by Christ:

> "Something which has existed since the beginning, that I have heard and I have seen with my own eyes, that I have watched and touched with my hand—the Word who is life—this is my subject. That life was made visible; I saw it and I am giving my testimony, telling you of the eternal life which was with the Father and has been made visible to me. What I have seen and heard, I am telling you so that you, too, may be in union with me as I am in union with the Father and with His Son, Jesus Christ. I am writing this to you to make my own joy complete." (1 John 1:1-4)

St. John did not hesitate to proclaim this to the early Christian community. He expressed it in the plural and, in truth, it is more accurate to use the plural because only *together* can we witness to the fulness of the mystery of Christ. Individually isolated, we can only give partial witness. By ourselves we are always forgetting and only together can we remember, can we give witness to the fulness of the mystery of Jesus.

Through the reality of the Sacraments Christ is always active in us, always going deeper into us. And, He is always creating something new and distinctive in response to the needs and the call of our own time. So, Evangelization is a constant call to listen, then to come and to go. That call is made and celebrated in the Eucharist. Eucharist means we have heard and have listened to the words of Christ each day—not words uttered over bread and wine, but evangelizing words begun over bread and wine and echoing over every person, over every nation. Words of consecration are words of evangelization. The Christian cannot celebrate Eucharist unless he goes also to his sister. The Eucharist is a sign that evangelization is going on, that we are evangelizing. The Eucharist begins with an admission, with a confession that I am responsible for evangelizing the world. Eucharist creates in us the capacity to be evangelized and evangelizers, to recognize that each person has a gift to give me, a work to do in me, a message to declare in me. Evangelization calls for unconditional love, which is to say, it calls for unconditional suffering. If one evangelizes, one cannot escape suffering. The very meaning of evangelization is to render oneself present even to those who do not choose us— and to continue to render ourselves present over and over again. We are sent and we are to create an environment of understanding and compassion. We are to create the possibility of other people becoming present to themselves. We are to become a center of communion, of community, where we cease to be anonymous, where we recognize one another, loving one another. It is difficult to comprehend how totally we are called to evangelize, to create family and kinship. Evangelization has already taken place in Jesus, yet so many have not experienced it. And this is our call, this is our mission—we are to make disciples, we are to make hearers, we are to create kinship. Evangelization begins with presence. We are taught presence through Eucharist—that we may render ourselves present to the people in our lives. Each one of us has an almost unbelievable power to evangelize, to create one another, to call forth life. Each of us is enough energy to change a city because He is with us!

Pope John Paul's emphasis on the unique, *unrepeatable* grace of each individual, of each person, is very significant. For, when we speak of evangelization, we speak of a new consciousness of the corporate call of the Church, which in a special way is the call of each individual by Christ to share in the Good News. Perhaps our deepest act of faith is to believe that we have His heart, His power to love and evangelize.

Each of us is capable of being evangelized by every person who enters into our lives because each one has the capacity to unfold to us that we are the image of God. Evangelization causes us to discover our own grace of presence to one another and our capacity to give life to one another, to the world. For a Christian there is no option—except to evangelize, to render oneself present to those to whom we are sent ... to the poor, the imprisoned, the oppressed. The closer one comes to people, the more one enters the mystery of Evangelization and the more inevitable it becomes to experience the pain of the people and the unity of the Eucharist. Because of the cumulative presence and growth of Jesus in us we are able to be with one another. We are disciples and thus evangelizers because we find ourselves in the same places He found Himself.

When you hear the word "evangelization," what comes to your mind? What is the first thought, the first word, the first association? When has evangelization happened to you? Who is the evangelizer of your life? Is it an idea or a person? An individual or a community? How dangerous, risky, is it? Some associations people have expressed to me are convert, member, muscular Christianity, triumphalism, embarrassment, too little-too late, presumption, arrogance, spiritual colonization ... and the litany goes on. With most people there is an immediate hesitancy, a certain kind of strangeness. Much of this fear, especially in the American Catholic Church, stems from our immigrant history. Most of our forebears came from pre-dominantly Catholic countries where any need for evangelization apparently had long disappeared. Until the middle of this century, Catholics in the United States were ethnic minorities striving to survive and to find acceptance among the dominant non-Catholic and secular culture. It was a question of survival, motivated by fear and anxiety, rather than a vision of expanding and enriching the dominant culture with the Good News of our faith, our way of life. Those caught in upward mobility do not easily lend themselves to prophetic witness of the Gospel. The new Catholic pluralism of post-Vatican II has softened the embarrassment of the Catholic. And now, one danger is that our faith can become so privatized, so personal, so intimate, that it earns the description of being timid and shy.

We are in the midst of an immense identity crisis because we have almost lost our distinctiveness. How easy it is today for a Catholic to take the journey into anonymity and oblivion. When there is no tension between believers and the secular culture, we are no longer Christian. When we no longer dare to stand up, to commit ourselves, we become anonymous Christians. Jesus called into existence a community of disciples to follow Him at extreme risk. A "safe" Christianity is not Christian. We can continue as Christians, as Catholics, only as a subculture. So if evangelization strikes us as novel and disquieting, these are some of the factors that make it a strange and alien concept for the American church.

One of my favorite descriptions of evangelization is that of one poor person helping another poor person to find bread— one beggar helping another beggar. Yet, evangelization refuses to be defined in an exclusive, once and for all, way. Beware of one line descriptions! Evangelization happens on many different levels and is a process that we are re-discovering now at this new moment in church history. We are all aware of evangelization as a missionary vocation, of going into far away places with strange sounding names—evangelization as some place out there. Now in a new, more direct way, we are called to a new kind of presence in the world. Families, parishes, institutions must strive for an effective way to reach out, to bring the Word of God to the community at large.

Essential to the very mission of the Church, evangelization must bring the Good News into all areas of humanity, so that through its influence, humanity will be transformed from within and made new. This incredible task is not going to be done in three years, thirty years or three hundred years! In two thousand years, we have not made that much of an indentation upon human consciousness. Yet, we must not become discouraged. Like Paul, we may be compelled to cry out, "Woe to me if I do not proclaim the Good News!"

Evangelization is threatening. Even so, in God's providence, NOW seems to be the time. His Spirit is always manifesting a new direction, a new kind of boldness, that does not come from ourselves. One of the great graces of Vatican II was an acknowledgment of our arrogance. Vatican II humbled us to see—we are on pilgrimage . . . we are searching . . . we are discovering. We thought we had it all together—what an illusion! We were what we could be at that time, but we were not the last word. Now, we are asking, "Do I live what I believe? Do I really preach what I live?" The witness of one's life has become, more than ever, an essential condition for real effectiveness if we are to invite others to share our faith. Precisely because of this, we are responsible for the progress of the Good News that we proclaim.

There is a ministry, a mysterious ministry in each of us. We do not know where it comes from, but it is there—that call in each of us which goes beyond our own heart. It is His call to pray in depth, His call to evangelization. You have been given the Holy Spirit in order to recognize that call already given to you. Prayer reveals there is something more. We are compelled by prayer to go out of ourselves. The prayer of the Christian becomes mysteriously entwined with Christ. Prayer in Christ, prayer in depth is evangelization. The root of evangelization is prayer. Our prayer-presence to Him becomes His compelling force in us to become present to others. We can know that we are living in Him and He is living in us because He lets us share His Spirit.

Each of us is a center of prayer, a center of evangelization. His Word dwells among us and goes out from us. Because we pray, we evangelize. All Christian prayer has mission in it. Evangelization is unfinished because the radical kind of prayer to which He calls us is still at a distance from us. Ultimately, the reason why a Christian prays is because Christ prays. The reason why a Christian evangelizes is because Christ does. "Go and teach." "Make disciples of every nation."

Evangelization presupposes internal conversion. When we ask questions like, "How many converts do we have? How many people are we converting?", we must also ask, "Is there an arrogance in presupposing that WE are already converted?" We must be very leery of the "ion" words that presume a state of life, that in some way imply that we have already arrived. The Gospel is always going to be new—a new reality is always happening in us. St. Paul in his letter to the Ephesians says:

"You must give up your old way of life; you must put aside your old self, which gets corrupted by following illusory desires. Your mind must be renewed by a spiritual revolution so that you can put on the new self that has been created in God's way, in the goodness and holiness of truth."

The paradox is that it is new because it is so old, it is fresh and alive because the roots go so deep.

Pope Paul has reminded us that,

"Fidelity both to a message whose servant we are and to the people to whom we must transmit it living and intact is the central axis of evangelization. It poses three burning questions: In our day, what has happened to the hidden *energy* of the Good News, which is able to have a powerful effect on man's conscience? To what extent and in what way is that evangelical *force* capable of really transforming the people of this century? What method should be followed in order that the *power* of the gospel may have its effect?"

Energy ... power ... and, force—can we become aware of the depth of these questions for us?

A radio commentator, almost as an aside, said that we are running out of our natural energy—gas, oil and coal—that we will have to develop the infinite sources of energy—the sun, the wind and the ocean. His statement was very incisive in terms of the Church today. As in our Lord's day, our way-of-being is that we rarely do anything that we do not have to do. So thank God for the crisis, thank God for the attrition, thank God that we have lost a little of our arrogance. And, thank God that a kind of new humbleness dwells in us, that we acknowledge that we do not know everything, that we do not have all the answers, that the Holy Spirit has yet some work to do in us! Work that always has to be done again and again and again. Evangelization is never completed once and for all. Perhaps that was our great illusion—that we could evangelize one generation and it would be passed on forever. Every generation has to begin anew.

The framework for evangelization is simply that Jesus is the

Evangelist. When I first began to prepare for Evangelization, I thought, "What kind of program will we need to do this? What kind of new structures? What kind of training and education? What kind of social service will be necessary?" Then I remembered that Jesus was not very successful as an evangelist—with his preaching, his miracles and even with his disciples. He was not successful, at least, as our culture considers success. Jesus' evangelization came out of the integrity of His life to His words, His action, His suffering, His love. He is always inviting us to follow. How free are we to be evangelizers?

"I am an evangelizer! Me . . . an evangelizer!" How did it happen? How does it continue to happen? There is a mystery attached to an evangelizer, something about an evangelizer which touches the personal identity of each person. The evangelizer is not just anyone. She carries the prophetic word and power; he is provocateur. She comes with Good News, points to something beyond, deeper; He is a dependent—depending on Jesus Christ and on the Christian community. The evangelizer is a person on a journey, a pilgrim, a small star in the darkness. The ever silent dialogue of faith is at the heart of the evangelizer's life. Jesus sends the evangelizer into the midst of people as His Father had sent Him.

If we are to be free to evangelize, we must become aware of the power of our culture upon us in regard to evangelization. For it is not an American success story. How humbling when we realize that the ultimate act of Jesus, his ultimate act of evangelization, was suffering and death. The primary evangelists down through the centuries have always been the martyrs and the saints. So, evangelization will never happen through any short term program. In Jesus' words, "I must proclaim the Good News of the Kingdom of God, that is what I was sent to do." One description of an evangelist is someone who discovers the truth of his or her life as a revelation that he or she is compelled to share with others, someone who has discovered the presence of Christ so deeply in their life that their life becomes transparent and they are compelled to share their life in Christ with others who are drawn to them because of the radiant joy that shines out of their being. Evangelization happens because of the permanence of Jesus' presence in the midst of his people. Jesus always remains the prime evangelist.

Evangelization depends on the daily Word of Jesus. The disciple of Jesus would not go a day without hearing that Word, letting it create him or her. The Word of God is not simply a word about Him. Every Word of God is a consecrating Word rendering Him present; and, it renders us present to ourselves and to Him. Evangelizing prayer radicalizes, frees. When one prays faithfully, individuals change because something happens when we live in His presence. Evangelizing prayer is a way of rendering ourselves present to ourselves, and out of that presence to enter into His presence and in His presence to be taken into the presence of the whole Christ. Our whole life must be an evangelizing prayer—not simply doing holy things, holy actions—but doing all things in the Spirit.

The effectiveness of evangelization depends on our experience of God, our experience of Jesus, not just theologically or rationally, but our coming to know Him experientially. And this takes time. Our experience of ministry, of evangelization has to be an experience of Him. Evangelization does not consist in what we leave of ourselves with others, but in what we leave of Him.

In order to grow in evangelizing prayer, one needs another person, someone to be brother or sister. Jesus never sent anyone out alone. He always sent disciples two by two. We need to rediscover the law of the Gospel and share our evangelization with someone who can be with us a center for discernment, decision and fidelity. We need someone to help us to be faithful, to be obedient to the grace of evangelization.

It is easy to be converted to Jesus, as long as He does not turn us into His people. And, the conversion to Jesus is but the first step in being the Body of Christ. We need to realize the reciprocal links between evangelization and the Church— for, the primary work of the Church is evangelization. The Church remains sign—a sign that is simultaneously obscure and luminous of a new presence of Jesus, of his departure and his permanent presence. The Church will always be an embarrassment, yet that does not diminish the reality that is hidden within it. This intimate life of Christ within the Church only acquires its full meaning when it becomes a witness, when it evokes admiration and conversion.

The first witness is the wordless witness, the irresistible questions stirred up in the hearts of those who see how Christians live. Such a witness is already a silent proclamation of the Good News—and, a very powerful and effective one. Here is an initial act of evangelization; here lies the test of truth, the touchstone of evangelization. A person simply cannot accept the Word and give himself or herself to the Kingdom without becoming a person whose life bears witness to it and proclaims it in turn.

There is a readiness in the hearts of the people of our time to hear the Word. An extraordinary process is manifested when someone proclaims the gospel by his or her life. The words of a true evangelist take root and open new depths of potential in the hearts of the listener. When our Lord sent his disciples out to witness and to heal, He sent them out before we would consider them ready. And, like us, they discovered a new depth of need for Him, if they were to be effective.

The evangelism of silent presence and witness is a kind of witness of punctuation. We not only proclaim, but we explain the gospel; we live in such a way that we are a question mark to others; and, we invite their questions, compel them to wonder at the joy and peace and compassion in our lives. The most dynamic evangelization is the witness of an authentic life in Christ. Modern man listens to witnesses more readily than to teachers. And, in truth, is there any other way of spreading the Good News then by transmitting to another person one's personal experience of faith?

Paul in his letter to the Ephesians prays, "May He give you the power through His Spirit for your hidden self to grow strong." What is that hidden call, that hidden presence in each of us? Evangelization is calling us to a new perception and a new understanding of what it is to be Christian. The family is the place where the Gospel is transmitted and from which the Gospel radiates. Every member of the family evangelizes and is evangelized. The parents communicate the Gospel to their children, and from their children they can themselves receive the same Gospel as lived deeply by them. So often the conversion that happens within children when they hear the Word uttered by their parents occurs at a deeper level than in the parents who uttered it.

Sharing the Good News is perhaps the simplest description of evangelization for us today. Sharing the Good News creates an awareness of reverence and humility—humility at having received the gift of the Good News while, at the same time, knowing that there is no one of us, or even all of us together, that make it that visible or that transparent or that attractive to the world. Yet, it is a sharing, a recognizing, that we receive something which we cannot hold onto ourselves, something which causes us to reach out in humbleness to others because it has meant so much to us.

We share Someone who is always new, who is present and presence with/in us. The Gospel is new only when it is new in our life, when it calls forth from us a joy, when it calls forth from us to other people an invitation of something good, meaningful, liberating, expansive, and life-giving. The Gospel makes us concerned for our own good and for the good of others. The Good News overflows from our life into the lives of others. Its message has become very personal to us. The core of the Christian Good News is not of knowledge, ideas or thoughts. Above all, we experience the Good News! We experience that God loves us intimately and personally.

Fear and anxiety are, perhaps, the most over-riding characteristics of this century. So the greatest word or experience that we are to make visible is that God loves us. God loves you; God loves me—that is tremendous news! God loves us with a universal and unconditional love. Jesus has united Himself with every person. Once this is experienced, new relationships are established and a whole new kind of presence to other people emerges. We are liberated from those fears which entrap and ensnare so many people.

Out of this experience with Jesus comes a community of servants who celebrate by drawing others into it. John Paul calls it a kingly service, the service of a king waiting upon us. Yet the question is, even though we have heard this message and attempt to live it out in our lives, can our neighbors hear this message? Can it be simply a matter of words? This is why justice is so imperative for our country, for our Church. There is no mid-ground between liberation and oppression. The person of Jesus—not the structure around him—is the central core of the message, of people who proclaim like Paul, "I know Him in whom I have believed."

Who are the evangelizers? Everyone is called by Jesus to proclaim the Good News. We are called to be people who live by Jesus, people in whose life we experience something of His presence. To live with the kind of presence that compels us to overcome fear, so that we are never afraid to affirm the presence of God. This presence creates in us a reverence and a humbleness before each person knowing that they, too, carry the hidden presence of Christ, knowing that as we reach out to another, we, too, are poor people who seek our Bread together.

Hope is a great virtue that the Spirit is breathing in us today—hope that is not something individual, isolated. The effect of Jesus in any person's life is to create new relationships with others, a new kind of communion with others. One of the most distinctive aspects of evangelization is that it calls for communities of evangelizers, not individuals in isolation. Alone each one of us is but a small fragment, only together can we reflect the mystery of Jesus.

We are essentially an incarnational people and the call to incarnate the whole message exists not simply in individuals, not simply in those called into religious communities, but every baptized person is called within small communities to be a minister of light to light, of prisoner to prisoner, of couple to couple. Each of us singly and together is to discover a common ministry based on the grace of the Spirit.

Yet, we ask, why? Why evangelize? Why should I be involved in this? Why? Because we believe that our message is unique. We believe that there will be many who will never come to know the God of Jesus Christ except through our presence. We believe that all people have been invited to a unique personal knowing of Jesus as the supreme gift of their life and that this personal knowledge increases their human existence, makes a difference in their humanity. We are called to become as human as Jesus. The knowledge and experience

of Jesus releases a whole new energy in the human person and
in human communities that will never be experienced without
Him. A relationship to God depends upon our knowledge and
relationship to Jesus in an ever new, personal and intimate
way. Evangelization happens because of a new excitement, a
new adventure and a new conviction of who Jesus is. Another
way of describing evangelization is that it is the process of
conversion, the process of a change that is never finished. We
can never think of ourselves as being totally converted. Yet,
we are on the way, we are in the process. The fulness of faith is
ahead of us, not behind us. We experience a change, a
metanoia, a conversion—individually, personally, socially—
that allows Christ to be the center of our life. Jesus becomes
decisive in the totality of my life.

We are undergoing a re-evangelization in communities in
whom the reality of Christ is fading or has been crowded out
by too many other things; we are undergoing a new con-
sciousness-raising in order that we can respond more adequately to the call and invitation of the day—an inculturation.
Basic Christian communities are emerging that witness to one
another and call forth and energize one another in faith, hope
and love.

Dialogue is always the basis of evangelization, a ministry of
friendship, a ministry of service, a ministry of concern so that
we know our neighbors and they know us. The renewal,
becoming evangelized ourselves, is more than simply hearing
the Word—the Word must be carried to a new depth within
us.

Fr. Walter Buhlmann, in his book *The Coming of the Third
World*, gives an example of a sister-doctor in Yemen who was
not allowed in any way to engage in evangelization. Yet, one
of her co-worker's could say of her, "I don't know why, but
when you are here the poor are better served." I don't know
why, but when you are here the poor are better served—that
was the only affirmation she received in three years. How
much it conveyed!

Evangelization is learning a language, a power, is learning
how to open doors. It demands a new way of perceiving
ourselves and the world around us. We become responsible

for the Gospel. If I am not a co-founder of the Church, then I am a confounder! Evangelization is to discover the uniqueness of His call, to become aware of a new sense of vocation, of mission, of being called and sent.

Becoming Catholic in the true sense of the word is to become universal brother and sister. The mission spirit is intrinsic to every Christian calling for/forth a charism of universal love. The Gospel was not a book in the early church, not a writing—the Gospel was a living person. Every one of us in some way is called to be that gospel and to value each of our meetings with others. What is the value of one person? Recently a woman wrote to me:

> " . . . how immune we have become to statistics! A friend was telling me of 50,000 individuals having been killed recently in a Central American country. He quoted it as if they were ants—and, he is not insensitive . . . it is that we have become so used to it! 50,000 individual conscious-nesses snuffed out—how long would it take to know just one thing about each one? 50,000 children of God murdered—for what? greed . . . power . . . adventure. What does this ask of me?
>
> Jesus cried over Jerusalem. Jesus cries over Nicaragua, Africa, Poland, the Philippines and on and on . . . and well He may! 50,000 people—is my heart big enough to love 50,000? Are there enough tears in our world to grieve such madness? Why doesn't God give up on us? And still, there are five billion people on Earth. Numbers are dangerous! What is 50,000 out of five billion? What can I do for you, Jesus?"

What is the value of one person? The silence and hiddenness of each individual is as mysterious, as secret, as wondrous as God's. If we but knew the gift of God and Who it is that lives in us!

We are each of us called to be a sacrament of salvation, a cause, a source and a proclamation. The Incarnation was the first mission. Christ was sent to do the work of the ministry as the Holy Spirit descended upon Him in prayer—and, incre-

dible as it may sound, the same Holy Spirit that brought forth
the Incarnation has been given to all of us. The word "mission"
really belongs to the Trinity in a unique way. Out of the
relationship and love of the Father to His son, the Son to the
Holy Spirit, we have been given: "As the Father has loved Me
so I love you; as the Father has sent Me, so I send you." Will
we ever live into an understanding of that reality?

Pope Paul VI, in speaking of the poor, said,

> "You are the mystery of the presence of Christ. The
> sacrament of the Eucharist offers us His hidden presence—
> living and real. You, too, are a sacrament, a sacred image of
> the Lord among us, as if it were a revealing, unconcealed
> reflection of a human and divine countenance and all the
> Church's tradition recognized in the poor the sacrament of
> Christ, a mystical correspondence with the Eucharist."

Jesus, as a sign that He was the Promised One, preached to
the poor. This indeed is the touchstone of evangelization—the
Good News is proclaimed to the poor—and not at a distance.
Jesus did not set himself up at a distance to wait for people to
come out to him. He went where they were and he proclaimed
it by His presence.

Some have raised the question: Who is ready for evangelization? Can anyone hear the Word of God unless one needs to
hear that Word? Perhaps only the poor can evangelize. We are
only beginning to explore the relationship of evangelization to
the poor. Perhaps only a few of us recognize how poor we are!
Without persecution, without an exodus, we have become the
remnant, a minority, a diaspora. We have lost our arrogance,
our triumphalism. Maybe we are becoming poor enough to
hear the Gospel! He is always faithful "for He can never disown
his own self." We may be the unfaithful people through whom
He continues to work. Only the poor can hear the Gospel,
only those who recognize their need for Him. How easy it is
for us who are affluent to insulate ourselves from the cry of the
vast majority of the world. Poverty is the grace which sinks us
deep into the mystery and work of evangelization. We become
poor to the degree that we experience His evangelizing presence

in us, to the degree that things no longer have power over us. Poverty is a sign of evangelization and a consequence of being in Christ.

The Gospel is revolution, a revolution which makes all other revolutions anemic by comparison. New light and energy are continually breaking through from the Gospel to us as light breaks through from distant stars never before seen. We become responsible for this new light and energy which compel us to see our society and way of life in new perspectives. When we least expect, Jesus interrupts our good life and cries out again. "The time has come and the Kingdom of God is close at hand. Repent, and believe the Good News!" And, evangelization begins again. The Gospel will always be new, always good! The most dangerous, yet most common, illusion is to believe that we are already evangelized, that we are Christian, that we are Gospel people. To think we have arrived is to feel that we no longer have to move, to grow. Jesus is always "going on ahead." We will always have to be in exodus, on pilgrimage. To be Christian is to live in tents, to be always breaking camp, to move from grace to grace, from metanoia to metanoia, from manna to manna, from Eucharist to Eucharist, from Nazareth to Jerusalem. Discovering Jesus is to discover those with whom He identifies—especially the least of His members. Meeting with Jesus is to enter into solidarity with the poor.

> "I tell you solemnly, insofar as you neglected to do this to one of the least of these, you neglected to do it to Me." (Mt 24:45)

This is the holy question, the holy confrontation of the Church today. Can anyone be truly human, can anyone be Christian, without identifying with the poor? Most of us do not know how to meet, speak, touch, live with the poor. Today, we might pray for the grace to recognize the poor as our evangelists, the ones closest to the Gospel, the ones who have refused to settle for anything less than Jesus.

An imperative of evangelization is justice. Justice comes from love, from suffering, from Eucharist. The evangelizing church, the Eucharist in all of its depth, can bring forth justice, render Christ present, render people present to Him and to one another. The ultimate witness of the reality of the evangelizing church is justice—the sacrament of evangelization. The church seeking justice today finds herself confronted, challenged, even attacked. The Gospel is intended to be a leaven in a fire. If you are not committed to justice, to evangelization, then you should not be celebrating the Eucharist. The voice of the oppressed seeking justice is as a mighty wind blowing over the Church.

Evangelization must confront the two capital sins of our culture: consumerism and individualism . . . greed and power. The more things we acquire, the more we cut off from one another and the more fearful we become of each other. We become so poor that we have to buy everything. Yet the most important human realities cannot be bought, collected or possessed by oneself in isolation. The deepest values are experienced only in sharing. How easily we insulate ourselves from the vast majority. We feel that we do not need to pray; we no longer hear the Gospel because we do not *need* the Gospel.

There is but one path to Jesus and it is the same path which He took to come to us. He emptied Himself of everything so that He became one with us. He told us where we could find Him—in the sacrament of the poor. How terribly poor and simple are His words, His disciples, His invitations, His final gifts to us: bread for the desert journey, wine for the dancing. Being poor does not necessarily lead to love, but love always leads to being poor. "Blessed are those who love enough to be poor." To become free for evangelization, we must become free enough to be poor, to be nothing.

Evangelization will never be possible without the action of the Holy Spirit. And, in the consolation of the Holy Spirit, the Church increases. The Holy Spirit is the Soul of the Church. The Holy Spirit today, just as in the beginning of the Church, acts in every evangelizer who allow himself or herself to be possessed and led by it. Techniques of evangelization are good, yet even the most advanced ones could not replace the gentle action of the Spirit. The Spirit alone stirs up the new creation. There is a beauty, a mystery, of going out even in our poverty.

No one must ask, "Are you weak enough? Are you poor enough to evangelize?" Rather we must ask, "Are you foolish enough to reach out in the fulness of Jesus?" The call of duty for those who hear the Word of God and try to live it is to invite, to draw, to awaken others to Jesus, who continues to dwell among us in love, and to the Holy Spirit, who will guide us, console us and even lead us to places we would rather not go. Yet, we go willingly and with confidence as long as we continue to dine with Him at His table! And, we shall sing with the psalmist of old:

> O sing to the Lord a new song;
>   sing to the Lord, all the earth!
> Sing to the Lord, bless his name;
>   tell of his salvation from day to day.
> Declare his glory among the nations,
>   his marvelous works among all the peoples!
>
> (Ps 96:1-3)

5

Free for the Prayer
that Leads to
Action for Justice

What is the distinctive kind of Christian prayer that inspires action for justice? What are the experiences of prayer that lead us to a new kind of presence which is an energizing power in us and in others? A religious woman responded in these words, "I'm not at all sure there is a prayer that inspires action for justice, and I am even less sure about the kind of action I would engage in without prayer."

Prayer is essentially a presence, a presence not easy to come by. An immense amount of energy is necessary to become present to oneself. How much easier it seems to live on the surface of life, absent from oneself and the essential depths of our being. Our age is an age of energy crisis; perhaps the greatest energy crisis is the personal and the community kinds of energy that are necessary to recreate our society. Prayer is a presence, an interactive kind of presence, an energizing power of interaction that creates compassion, empathy, sensitivity.

Those who struggle with this question are usually people of middle-class experience. The poor do not have such luxury. We begin by recognizing the accident of being educated, and to be humbled by that fact and that challenge. Prayer is a mystery of the Spirit giving witness to my spirit. Prayer demands discovery of who I am and a recognition that everything I have is gift. Prayer creates an honesty with oneself and with God; prayer develops a reverence before the mystery of one's neighbor, especially the poorest of the poor. Prayer is focused on people—not on an abstraction.

One of the oldest dimensions of prayer is to recognize one's poverty, one's incapacity, one's inability to make a difference. To recognize that all that happens must be the work of God and not of myself is to face the embarrassment of being an "unprofitable servant." Prayer purifies in us a willingness to work for nothing, to be "good" for nothing. This awareness, this humility and this honesty before oneself is an acceptance and a recognition of one's limitations ... an acknowledgment we need, lest we burn out and become embittered. Clem Kern, a priest in Detroit, taught us his secret of prayer—his attitude of *affirming* others was that he seemed to expect nothing from them. And with no expectations, he was always surprised and delighted by anything that happened. The most subtle oppression is the imposition of one's expectations on another.

This prayerful attitude leads to the discovery of our own poorness, and that frees us to be poor. Out of this poorness, out of this need, comes a deeper need—a demand for community. We are led to the realization that we must reflect, analyze, evaluate and motivate together. Prayer demands a continuous study in order to see one's world clearly; for, that which is closest to one's self is usually the last reality to be recognized. Prayer needs community reflection and celebration. Goodwill is not enough. Immediate service without understanding of the whole situation usually creates chaos. Compassion does not come easy. More than a matter of words, compassion is a matter of being close enough to hear people's pain. With each step we take in our poverty to build the Kingdom, the more God is revealed to us.

Why has it taken us so long to look at the roots of oppression? A new dimension of justice is drawing us. We have an immense freedom that we have been afraid to live— we are free to change, we are free to build a new world. Building the Kingdom with free people—not with words—is the truest revelation of God. God's presence is dimmed by injustice and oppression. The time to recognize this is NOW.

In my years in an inner city parish, I have been struck most by the incredible faith of people. My own faith has always been deeply affirmed. I have every reason in the world to believe; I have unlimited evidence for that faith. I am astonished again and again by people who have no reason to believe, no evidence—yet, they continue to believe. And, I question who is poor and who is rich. Discovering my own poverty is to discover the door of the poor's richness, that they have been compelled to develop everything that they have. There is so much of me, so much of us, that has never had to be developed because it was never called forth. Oppression creates its own reverse power until eventually, like a huge metal spring compressed too far, it releases a tremendous energy. We have a heritage of persecution, and perhaps the greatest illusion of our day and of our church is that we do not recognize the oppression in our midst. We do not recognize that when anyone is oppressed, it is God's presence that is oppressed. When one person is diminished, all of us are affected. The more we struggle for justice, the more God is revealed.

Prayer ultimately inspires action for justice, yet perhaps the most immediate way is through pain and anguish. Many people have come to compassion, to a new kind of presence, through pain and through trauma. The two immediate responses to pain and trauma are either to escape by flight or to suppress or erase. We have an awesome capacity, not only as individuals, but as a community and as a whole church, to suppress and to erase that which we cannot face. As we deepen in our prayer life, we develop an ability to accept pain and anguish and to live with a heightened consciousness, a new sensitivity, a new hope.

I saw this most vividly in South Africa among the Blacks who were interned and tortured. Those who survived came through with an incredible hope and a serenity that was almost beyond belief. Something happens in Christians with deep faith that enables them to handle suffering in a way that is inexplicable to the secular world. I remember talking in South Africa to women in a contemplative community who had been so traumatized by the violence around them that they were ready to take to guerilla warfare. Yet some of the Blacks who had been through torture had a redemptive compassion;

they did not hate. For the first time, I realized that there is a violence in each of us that must be overcome if one is to truly act justly.

Steve Biko, a martyr of South Africa, dared to say justice is not enough; for Christians, justice must lead to reconciliation. Perhaps even for Jesus, who often uttered violent words against the Pharisees, it was only through His agony of the Cross that He could finally say, "Forgive them, for they do not know what they are doing." The most powerful witness to the presence of the Spirit will always be to love one's enemies.

Justice is one of the most demanding challenges to us to become free, to enter into a heritage of the Abrahamic journey. "Leave all that you have and go into a new country." The journey that is being asked of us is not a journey into the desert; rather, it is a journey out of where we have been. It is a journey to relocation. It is a journey of redistribution, a journey of reconciliation.

One truth that we are only now beginning to recognize is that we are not free to preach the gospel because we are not free to be poor. We do not know how to leave our cultural condition and go into a new environment, to relocate ourselves so that we can be present, so that we can release the hidden energy within ourself to free those who sit in darkness and the shadow of death. This is the prayer, the community, the redistribution, the relocation that can bring the reconciliation that leads to the justice of God, of His holiness and His integrity.

Today's justice is interwoven with structure, with institutions, with systems. Justice is political; it is public and includes the personal, the interpersonal, the systemic. Paul wrestled with this same problem in the early Christian community when he urged the reconciliation of the Jews and pagans with one another. Today we must speak about the reconciliation of the church with the poorest of the poor.

> "Do not forget, I say, that you had no Christ and were excluded from membership of Israel, aliens with no part in the covenant, with their promise; you were immersed in the world without hope and without God. But now in Christ Jesus, you that used to be so far apart from us have been

brought very close by the blood of Christ. For He is the peace between us, and has made the two into one and broken down the barrier which used to keep them apart, actually destroying in his own person the hostility caused by the rules and decrees of the Law. This was to create one single new person in himself out of the two of them, and by restoring peace through the cross, to unite them both in a single Body and reconcile them with God." (Eph 2:12-16)

Thus, the Jews and pagans were brought together. The pagans of our day are the poor, or maybe it is we who are the pagans. Perhaps, the only ones who can evangelize are the poor. Only the poor are free enough to respond to the gospel. Perhaps only the poor have ears to hear the gospel. Most of us have let go of the gospel along with the first Beatitude—"Blessed are the poor, for they have not settled for anything else." If we settle for anything else, then we let go of the gospel. We become comfortable in our bondage.

We are called to a new kind of accountability, a new kind of discernment, a new kind of redistribution, relocation and reconciliation. We are called once again to read the gospels in a new way, to be drawn to a higher level of consciousness, to know that revelation is not finished.

The words of the gospel are elusive. His words are always "too much." We are always forgetting the Word which is too penetrating. And so, time and time again, we erase it, suppress it. The great call of the liturgy is to re-member again and again and again, because we are always being dis-membered. We can never hear the gospel adequately by ourselves. We need community. We need the incarnation of that Word into our lives. We have to see it enfleshed. The gospel is always beyond us. No one ever really catches up to the gospel. No matter what we hear in the gospel, it simply opens us deeper to what we have not yet heard. The gospel demands a freedom that few of us are ready for, a personal liberation movement in each of us. Remember that old Irish prayer—"May your first miracle be yourself." Each one of us is in need of a radical conversion—to be free to love, to be free to change, to be free to be poor, to find the place where we can truly experience Beatitudes lived.

Our Lord was not describing a future. He looked around and described what He saw. The Beatitudes are absurd. They make no sense—that is the whole point of the Beatitudes. Jesus does not make a demand in terms of where we are. He is always calling us out of where we are into a new place . . . a new kind of consciousness, a new presence with ourself, with others and with Him.

There is no way of being a disciple of Jesus unless we enter into His journeys. The journey we forget so often is the journey of Jesus in becoming poor. The Incarnation, the *kenosis*—the total emptying out of Jesus in becoming poor—is to journey to our brothers and sisters who are most deeply united with Him. The greater the love, the deeper the capacity to seek the last place, the lowest place. What immense love is necessary to be able to take the last place! The journey of Jesus in Eucharist—of all the ways Jesus could have continued His presence among us, the least likely and least significant would be to continue with us under the form of food and drink . . . the most unlikely of all. Do we really recognize how poor the Eucharist is? How absurd, how irrelevant. Remember, it was over the Eucharist that our Lord's own disciples balked at going any further. "Many of His disciples no longer walked with Him" at that point. From the very first moment of that journey into the emptiness and barrenness of the Eucharist, there was a crisis.

Yet that Eucharist was not an end; it was but the first step to the incredible mystery of His indwelling in us. The mystery of Jesus saying,

> "I will come to you, and my Father will come to you, and We will make our home in you." (Jn 14:23)

Each of these incarnational journeys is more radical and more incredible than the previous one. The most incredible journey of all is that He has chosen us to be His home. And whatever He has done, He asks us to do even more.

There is no greater poverty than the Incarnation. It would have been enough if He had but left His Word. It is almost too much for us that He leaves us His body and blood under the form of bread and wine. Most incredible of all is that He identifies Himself with us, the poorest of the poor, the privileged ones of Jesus.

The Beatitudes are a revelation of where Jesus is and will be. His command, "Where I am, I want you to be," is not simply an end-time invitation; it is where Jesus has been found down through the years. Where did Paul find Him? Paul found Him in the people he was oppressing. And we will find Jesus in the people whom we are oppressing. We have to admit that there is an oppressor in all of us—the middle-class, priests, religions . . . just by the fact that what we have, we have held to ourselves. Only Jesus is not an oppressor and we have not followed Jesus fully. And in not following Him we have diminished His light and His presence. The clearer the gospel is proclaimed, the fewer who will be ready to receive it. The more we understand what the gospel is all about, the more we will become a minority. We will be a little flock. The only true Christians are little brothers, little sisters, universal people.

Years ago at a retreat house, a woman wrote out a sentence on a scrap of paper and gave it to me. Sometimes people do things and you do not understand; it may take years to understand. She wrote, "There's no point in being Irish if you do not know that life will break your heart." I thought to myself, well, thanks a lot for nothing! Yet I carried that paper for fifteen years in my New Testament. Sometimes we hear something we cannot put into words, yet we know it is significant. Sometimes we have to carry a word a long time before it speaks to us. I have come to know how true that word is. For, there is no point in being Christian if you do not know that life will break your heart.

Suffering, pain and anguish are unavoidable in the human condition, yet every identification with Jesus must be free. There is a kind of suffering, a kind of anguish, that only Christians will ever suffer. There is a kind of compassion that only those identified with Jesus will ever know. There is a kind of reconciliation that does not happen except because He is present.

Again and again, the disciples came to Jesus and said that

what He was asking them was impossible. He never backed away from that. It is only when we come to the point in our human life where we experience the radically impossible that we begin to realize what Jesus is all about. What is *kenosis*, emptying out, relocation? If anyone ever made a relocation, imagine the relocation and dislocation of God becoming human! We have hardly begun to understand what Incarnation, what identification is. Charles de Foucauld, called the universal brother by Paul VI, came to the conviction that our reduction to nothing is the most powerful means we have of uniting ourselves to Jesus and doing good for souls. This is strange language to us, especially in our culture. We are so geared to achievement, to doing something, to becoming someone, to having something to show for our life.

As an epilogue to *The Seven Storey Mountain*, Thomas Merton wrote what may be prophetic for us, for our church, for the Christian community:

"For I am beginning to understand. You have taught me, and have consoled me, and I've begun again to hope and learn. I hear you saying to me, 'I will give you what you desire. I will lead you into solitude. I will lead you by the way that you cannot possibly understand, because I want it to be the quickest way. Therefore, all the things around you will be armed against you to deny you, to hurt you, to give you pain; and therefore, to reduce you to solitude. And because of their enmity you will soon be left alone. They will cast you out and forsake you, reject you, and you will be alone. Everything that touches you shall burn you, and you will draw away your hand in pain, until you have withdrawn yourself from all things. Then you will be all alone. . . . You will be praised and it will be like burning at the stake. You will be loved and it will murder your heart and drive you into the desert. You will have gifts and they will break you with their burden; you will have pleasures of prayer and they will sicken you, and you will fly from them. And when you have been praised a little, and loved a little, I will take away all your gifts, and all your love, and all your praise. And you will be utterly forgotten and abandoned, and you will be nothing, a dead thing, a rejection. And in that day you will begin to possess the solitude you have so long desired. And your solitude will bear immense fruit, and the souls of people you will never see on earth . . . you shall taste the true solitude of my anguish and my poverty. And I shall lead you into the high places of my joy, and you shall die in me and find all things in my mercy which has been created in you for this end . . . that you may become the brother of God and learn to know the Christ of the burnt men.'"

What a prophecy! Most of us are not called to that kind of experience. Yet I think it describes the passion of Christ and His body, the Church today. A choice is offered and it depends upon each one of us how far we wish to follow. Contact with the Mertons of the world activates something within us; for there is implanted in each of us a capacity to be like Jesus. Baptism infinitely capacitates us to be sons and daughters of God. There is enough energy in the least of us to change a world turned upside down. Faith in God is very demanding; even more demanding is faith in ourselves—faith that God's love is at work in us, belief that Christ's hidden power is at work within us. It is the journey of believing that each of us is prophet, evangelist. It is the journey of discovering that there is a truth in us so exciting that, once we begin to taste it, we are compelled to share it with others. It is the journey of celebrating that each one is the mystery of Jesus. So that when we are asked who He is, we dare to say, "I am."

One step in this direction is Jesus' invitation to pray always. What does it mean to pray always? We have the capacity to touch God; we have the capacity to experience Jesus, Yet first, we must develop our senses for God's mind and discipline. We must claim the freedom that is our birthright—not simply to do, but to be . . . to be in a state of prayer. Although we cannot always be saying prayers, we can always be receptive. We can be listening. We can expose ourselves again and again to His Word, until it so imprints us that we cannot forget it, until the after-image becomes constant. We will never know our identity until we come in contact with Him in whose image, in whose life we have been made, and toward whom, with the whole gravitational pull of life, we are moving.

Have you ever had that uneasy feeling of someone looking at you in a way that most people do not look at you? Jesus is always looking at us. His look is a discovery of ourselves. Certain people look at us and we experience ourselves in a way we have never known before. When Jesus looks at us, we are recreated. We discover who we are; we discover a new possibility. Jesus' look is always a mirror of something that we never knew existed in ourselves, something that He loves into us. This ministry of Jesus' looking at us and calling us is there from the very first moment of our existence. No one understands Jesus' call to them until it has been completed.

"How do you know me," as Nathanael was to discover, is the beginning of a great journey of knowing how intimately Jesus is in us and with us. He invites us to exercise in a very simple faith, hope and love, the root of which we rarely touch. Our faith and hope and love is not so much directed towards God, as it is discovering how much God believes in me, hopes in me and loves me. It is God's action far more than mine. Our faith and hope and love is the return on that laser beam way He touches us.

The simple exercise of faith, hope and love is prayer. What is prayer? Prayer is becoming present to myself, to the gift of myself that He has given me, to His presence in me. Prayer is the remembering, the thanksgiving, the recognition of the cumulative deposit of His word, of His sacrament, of His presence in me. Prayer is that new kind of interactive presence. The more I am in touch with the something more than myself, in myself, the more I become aware of that something more in the other person. The burning bush is not outside myself; I am that burning bush.

The purpose of every sacrament is to make us sacrament, to discover the hidden power at work in us. The hymn of the universe, the hymn of every person, is always drawing us into a prayer of thanksgiving. Only the poor can pray, only those who recognize that everything is gift. The more we recognize that all is gift and the poorer we become, the more we live in thanksgiving, in gratitude ... and, the more we are ready to give and to recognize the gift that is given. The more we can genuflect the heart—the bow of the spirit—the more we lift up our heads and are whole persons. We lift up our eyes and hearts and see. We have only to recollect at any given moment who and whose we are to encounter the God who is in dialogue with us, indeed whose dialogue we are. We are the Word of God that He never stops uttering. We are a presence of God ... we are sacrament.

We will never know how to pray as we ought, because everything is fragmented except in our inner depths where He dwells. Divine prayer can penetrate the gaps. We become the incense of prayer that reaches all the way to God; to let Him make so deep an impression on us that we remember Him in the midst of the world and see Him everywhere; to know that His spirit is always in us, always praying, that there is in the world a total word of assent, that our fragmentary prayer is included within the complete and incessant prayer of Jesus in our midst and in our depths. There is no point in being Christian if one does not know that life will break one's heart. But if our heart is not broken, we remain alone. Only to the degree that our heart is broken is there room for Him to come. And when He comes, He brings the whole world with Him.

If you choose, be quiet for a few moments and listen to your own response, your own reflection. What is the mystery of Jesus in you? How is He answering your question, "How do you know me?" What are you beginning to experience of that hidden presence, that hidden power in you? We are confronted with the unspoken question, "Are you the one we have been waiting for or must we wait for another?" Do you believe that you are the promised one? Do you believe you are the one that we have been waiting for? Do you believe that you are a new revelation? Do you believe in the power at work in yourself?

Simone Weil, that unforgettable young French philosopher, knew something of this when she wrote:

"God waits patiently until at last I'm willing to consent to love Him. God waits like a beggar who stands motionless and silent before someone who will perhaps give Him a piece of bread. Time is God's waiting as a beggar for our

love. The stars, the mountains, the sea and all the things
that speak to us of time convey God's supplication to us. By
waiting humbly, we are made similar to God. God is only
the good. That is why He is waiting there in silence. Anyone
who comes forward and speaks is using a little force. The
good which is nothing but good can only stand waiting.
Beggars who are modest are images of Him. Humility is a
certain relation of the soul to time. It is an acceptance of
waiting. ... God has left us abandoned in time. God and
humanity are like two lovers who have missed the ren-
dezvous. Each is there before the time, but each at a different
place, and they wait and wait and wait. Each stands motionless, nailed to the spot, for the hold of time. She is distraught
and impatient, but alas for her, she gets tired and goes
away. For the two places where they are waiting are at the
same point in the fourth dimension. The crucifixion of
Christ is the image of the fixity of God. God is attention
without distraction. One must imitate the patience and
humility of God."

What is the struggle for prayer that leads to action for
justice? We have reflected about the universal prayer that
happens in us no matter what faith or what condition or what
place we are. We have reflected about uniqueness of Christian
prayer, of the Incarnation, that Christ has made a difference,
that we are called to an incredible reality, to become as human
as Jesus is human. We have reflected upon the mystery of
what action, community, and the violence of our times do to
us. We have tried in some way to reflect upon the mystery and
sacrament of ourselves. All of these are but preludes to the
answer that Jesus Himself gives to us, to the question of our
day, "What is it that leads to and that inspires action for
justice?" It is nothing less than Jesus!

The Eucharist is the core prayer of every Christian; and, the
Catholic tradition has a unique power, a unique revelation, to
lead and to inspire action for justice. Yet we are still retarded,
we are still beginners in trying to understand what Eucharist
is. The commands of Jesus, the imperatives of Jesus, like His
questions, are always revelations of hidden power within our-

selves. There is nothing more for Him to give; there is nothing more for Him to say. All that He could have said, all that He could have given, is already with us. The Holy Spirit is given to us in order that we may come to understand the gift we have already received.

Jesus says, (cf. Jn 14)

> "I am the way, the truth, and the life. No one can come to the Father except through me. . . . I tell you most solemnly, you who believe in me will perform the same works I do myself. You will perform even greater works, because I am going to the Father. If you ask for anything in my name, I will do it. . . . I shall ask the Father and He will give you another Advocate to be with you forever: the Spirit of truth whom the world can never receive since it neither sees nor knows him. But you know him because he is with you; he is in you. I will not leave you orphans; I will come back to you. In a short time the world will no longer see me, but you will see me because I live, and you will live also. On that day you will understand that I am in my Father, and you in me, and I in you. You who receive my commandments and keep them, will be the ones who love me; and you who love me will be loved by my Father. And I shall love you and *show myself to you*. . . . If you love me, you will keep my word, and my Father will love you, and we shall come to you and make our home with you."

Ten lines from the fourteenth chapter of John's gospel. Where did John get this understanding? How did he come to it? It was almost too much; it was a suspect gospel for many decades.

Ultimately, there is only one prayer a Christian can pray. All prayer of a Christian is contemplative. There is no other way to pray. And there is no prayer of a Christian alone. The Eucharist is a corporate mystical experience. By mystical I mean that it is hidden. In fact, the more we attempt to penetrate it, the more hidden it becomes. One of the gifts of knowledge is to expand the understanding of our own ignorance. The great unfolding of our time is a new sense of the depth, and breadth and height of what Christ is doing in us, with us and through us. By listening to the words of John's gospel, we are invited into a new depth and height of consciousness.

How did John come to know the Jesus of his gospel? How did Paul come to know Jesus out of his initial communities, his missionary communities? The synoptic gospels are easy to understand; not as easy to understand is the origin of Paul's theology or of John's mysticism. Yet John and Paul are archetypes for today. The synoptic gospels could be called descriptive meditations. They are reflections, observations of the Christian community's experience. The only way John could have come to his gospel is out of the depth of contemplation. He opened himself so deeply and so profoundly that he became a whole new medium in which Jesus could express Himself. Every one of us is invited to be a similar medium, an instrument by which Christ continues His revelation, by which Christ continues the reality of the truth, truth that releases the immense energy and power so necessary to redeem and to liberate our contemporary world. Each one of us is invited to listen with the heart of John.

At the Last Supper, Jesus gave the imperative: "Do this in memory of me." How does one do Eucharist? In the third world countries, one often hears, "Can there be Eucharist without justice?" So often we get caught in holy lies, in sacred lies and holy actions that betray the truth one is attempting to express. Some even dare to say that an act of Eucharist is close to blasphemy when there is no justice. It is a contradiction, a lie. Perhaps those words are too strong, too violent; yet, in some way, they hint at the Eucharist as a terribly serious action. And each one of us has to ask ourself in new ways, where am I in the Eucharist? Is the Eucharist really the source and culmination of my prayer? Is it really prayer? "Be very careful what you teach them, they may learn it"—the danger of celebrating Eucharist without faith, without justice, without love.

The command of Jesus is to "do this in memory of me." We know that Jesus is faithful to his promise. It is not a question of the "real presence;" He will always be with us. The question today is much more of *our* presence. To what degree are we present to Christ? Are we present to the gospel? Are we present to the body of Christ? This is an essential question of mission and of ministry—what kind of presence?

We can now recognize many modalities of His presence: Christ is present in His word, in the Christian community, in His ministers, in the Eucharist. And the most intense presence of Christ remains Eucharist. To celebrate Eucharist is to remember His reality so intensely that He is compelled to render Himself present. The Eucharist is not simply a presence of Jesus. He is present in order that we might be present, that we might be empowered, that we might be energized in a way we could never be of ourselves.

How do you do Eucharist? What difference does your presence make? What difference does your life make to your Eucharist, and what difference does the Eucharist make to your life? These are not merely theological questions; these are questions of radical spirituality. These are questions of energy, of power. These are questions of conversion, of the ultimate reverence for God, questions of adoration—or of blasphemy. Is there anything more serious than what happens in Eucharist, which is really the question of what happens in us? If only the bread and wine is changed and nothing happens in us, is that not a contradiction of the Eucharist? The Eucharist is Christ's ultimate act of abandonment. The Incarnation was the first journey of Jesus into poorness, for God to become human. The second journey to Eucharist was a journey that was necessary because He could not come directly into us. Jesus took on the poorness of the Eucharist.

Gandhi once said, "The only way God could dare come to our door would be under the form of bread." There is no other way for Him to go, no other way for Him to come. But He has come under the form of bread to us in order that we can choose, in order that we can be free to choose Him, and to choose one another. Jesus could not say over John and Peter, "You are my body, you are my blood." Jesus could not consecrate them. Jesus could not pour Himself into them. Jesus stands at the door and knocks, and only when we open to Him can He come in.

The Eucharist is the way we open ourselves to Christ, and the way we open ourselves to all of those whom He brings to us. How do we render ourselves present? What will we do on the night before we die? What would we ever ask anyone to do in remembrance of us? What would you ask your friend to do in memory of you? Jesus summed up His whole life that evening, when it was dark, when it was night. No one ever died more freely than Jesus because no one ever loved more freely than Jesus. The Eucharist is a sacrament of freedom; it is a sacrament of decision; it is a sacrament of abandonment. It is the ultimate prayer—the only prayer any Christian can pray.

When the disciples came to Jesus and the crowds were hungry, they told Him to send the people away. They did not have the courage to do it themselves. And in that moment Jesus said, "Give them something to eat—yourselves." He told them then and at the Last Supper He showed them. He gave them something to eat. "This is my body given for you; this is My blood to be shed for you. Take and eat, take and drink." There is no other way of being Christian except in the degree that we love that freely and die that totally. The Eucharist will always be ahead of us. And this is why we come back again and again to be re-rooted, to experience the mirror of who He is, and who He calls us to be.

It has taken all of human history, scientific history, to crack the atom, in fission, in fusion, to release the immense energy in the smallest particle of matter. Once that is done the radiation lasts almost indefinitely. Plutonium radiation continues for 24,000 years. It is only in our day that we find a language that comes out of our technology to help us to believe the reality that we have carried with us for so long a time. What difference did Christ's love make so long ago? Can it still have power today? Does it still make a difference? Two thousand years is nothing. If a material particle has a radiation of 24,000 years, what can spiritual energy do? How long will it take to crack open our hearts? How much love will be necessary to heal another person? How long will it take truth to penetrate the human mind and heart, for the mystery of Incarnation, of Eucharist, of ministry to make a difference in us?

Human presence is an awesome power. Human presence can heal or destroy. There is no neutral kind of presence.

Either we are loving or we are hating, we are reverent or we are violent. By a look, we can diminish a person or increase them. What difference does your presence make upon Jesus? How much do we allow Him to be present in us in the world? How does His presence inspire our action, our energizing presence for others, for justice, for mercy, for truth? When you go into a church before the Blessed Sacrament, do you ever think of your presence making a difference in Christ's presence? Does He become more or less present because you are there? When you are alone in your room and someone enters, do you become more present to yourself or less present? There are some people in whose presence we are expanded, and others in whose presence we are contracted. Every person either expands us or diminishes us, and we carry that same power with us to one another.

In a letter to 400,000 priests, John Paul II wrote,

> "The ministerial priesthood is subordinated to the common priesthood of all Christians. The fundamental work of the ministerial priesthood is to activate the priesthood in the people of God."

Where is your priesthood? Where is your identification with Christ? When Eucharist is celebrated, who celebrates Eucharist most deeply, most freely?

In every Eucharist our incredible belief is that Christ renders Himself present. It really does not make any difference who the particular minister is, how sinful or how holy he might be. Christ always renders Himself present, because the Christian community believes in that reality. The point of the Eucharist is not simply the presence of Christ, but how does each one of us allow Him to be present in us and present in the world.

How does one do Eucharist? How does one enter into the action of Christ? How does one consecrate one's self? How does one make the decision freely to love and to die? The Eucharist is the ultimate act of human freedom. Only those who own themselves, give themselves. Christ was the freest human who ever lived. In one moment, He could give the totality of Himself forever and the power of that action has never ceased, never diminished. We only possess ourselves a moment at a time. We can speak for so little of ourselves; yet it is only what we give of ourselves to Him that He can use. Christ renders Himself present; He renders all of ourselves given to Him present in His Eucharist. He gives us the incredible gift to render Him present in word, in truth, in our lives wherever we are. St. Augustine said the gift that He gives to us in coming to us in Eucharist is not simply Himself, but ourselves. "See what you are, become what you see."

Do you really believe that you are called by God? If you were around in His day, would you have been one of those who followed Him? Would he have called you by name? Do you find more and more evidence that He has called you—and caught you? His work in us is to proclaim that He has come to us, He has made His home in us and we are to do even greater things than He has done. That in Him we have immense power to energize one another, to call forth that hidden power and to live it! That has been a secret through all generations. The treasure of the gospel remains hidden even in us who know ourselves to be the ones invited to proclaim it, to make it real, to make it tangible, to make it enfleshed. No one celebrates Eucharist by one's self, not even the priest. Ultimately the fullest way Eucharist can be understood is as a corporate mystical experience. By ourselves we are always forgetting—only together can we remember.

Each one of us is but a fragment of the totality of what Christ is. Yet each one of us as we come together can activate the hidden presence of Jesus in one another. Faith is a radiant power, so is hope and so is love. Prayer has a radiation that touches and intensifies one another. Imagine the immense power that is in one of the atomic plants. What might happen if there was some kind of a positive radiation? Imagine if you were exposed to a radiation that made you a year younger or ten pounds lighter. Imagine a radiation that would make you happier, more joyful. Imagine that there was some kind of radiation that would make you altruistic, that would make you concerned for others, that would free you from so many things that you thought were important. Imagine that there was some kind of a healing radiation. Imagine if something like that existed. Well it has—for two thousand years!

What if the Resurrection really happened? Do you ever think about that? What if it really happened? What if Jesus really is divine? What if He really is acting in your life? Every once in a while we should shock ourselves with that possibility. What if it is all true? What if it really is true? Well, that is what we proclaim when we celebrate Eucharist. We believe that Jesus is with us. He takes on the dimensions and coloration of each one of us and He knows each one of us by name. Each one of us has an incredible power to render Him present. Each one of us has a power to enable other people to be present to themselves. Imagine the energy in Jesus—the kind of ministry He did which was simply His presence, how much life He gave to everyone He knew, to everyone who touched Him.

At the Last Supper Jesus said, (cf. Jn 15)

> "All that I have learned from my Father, I have made known to you. All that I have received, I have handed over to you. As the Father has sent me, so I send you. As the Father has loved me, so I love you."

The ultimate power of the Eucharist is to dare when we are asked, "Who is Jesus?" to answer, "I am. He lives in me and I live in Him" ... to make known this mystery that has been hidden from all generations and is now revealed.

John joyfully expresses this mystery in his first epistle:

> "Something which has existed since the beginning that I have heard and I have seen with my own eyes; that I have touched with my own hands. The word who is light, this is my subject; that light was made visible; I say it and I am giving you my witness, telling you of the eternal light that was with the Father, and has been made visible, tangible to me. What I have seen and heard I am telling you so that you too may be in union with me, as I am in union with the Father, and with the Son, Jesus Christ. I am saying this to you to make my own joy complete."

The ultimate Christian prayer, the prayer that leads to action for justice, is the presence of Jesus, so alive in us that others experience that He is here. In their own language they cry out, "Alleluia, the Lord is here, praise Him!" To be Christian, to be missioner, to be people of the Eucharist, each of us must write our own letter, our own gospel in our hearts. Others will then hear it in their hearts.

6

Free to be Embarrassed by the Poor

"The word of God is living and active, sharper than any two-edged sword, piercing to the division of soul and spirit, of joints and marrow, and discerning the thoughts and intentions of the heart. And before God no creature can hide, but all is open and laid bare to the eyes of the One we answer to." (Heb 4:12-13)

"Being Christian" is often more easily understood as a factual description rather than a cautious presumption, a direction to be pursued, an immense journey which is hardly begun. We think that we are Christian and that the Church is proclaiming and living the fullness of the Gospel. Then, someone asks an innocent question like, "Where are the poor?" or, what is even more embarrassing, "Why are you not poor?" The Gospel always remains dangerous because someone will always be listening. Those in ministry and teaching must be very cautious. "Be very careful of what you teach them, they may learn it." What is more embarrassing than to be quoted back your own words with a power they did not have when they left you. The Word of God, as it falls into the hearts of some people, comes back with thirty, sixty, a hundredfold power and ramification!

When the "non-Christian" third world asks Gospel questions to the more "Christian" first world, a painful question arises. Where are Gospel values lived more faithfully, more consistently? Many observers affirm that the Gospel values of community, of love, of sharing, of poverty, of simplicity, are lived far more truly, more transparently, in the third world countries.

The grace of the Christian community is that we remain vulnerable to Gospel values no matter how long or how deeply we are seduced by the values of our consumer culture and lifestyle. We never know when we will be pierced by a word of the Gospel, especially when it comes from a non-believer.

> "Whoever of you does not renounce everything, cannot be my disciple." (Lk 14:33)

> "Though he was rich, yet, for your sake, he became poor, so that by the example of his poverty, you, too, might become rich." (2 Cor 8:9)

As I file a report on my stolen car, I remember, "Do not ask for your property back from anyone who robs you" (Lk 6:30). Just after having someone else handle the stranger at the door, I read, "Give to anyone who asks and if anyone wants to borrow, do not turn that one away. Lend without any hope of return" (Lk 6:35). These are not easy imperatives. They do violence to common sense and experience. Yet these words cannot be ignored. Too much of the Gospel reinforces them

> "For where your treasure is, there will your heart be also." (Lk 12:34)

> "If you are not able to do a small thing, why worry about the rest?" (Lk 12:26)

How long does it take for a Gospel value to penetrate the insulated layers of traditional conscience? We seem a long way from *metanoia*, yet the threshold has been pierced. In many, an awkwardness and embarrassed consciousness is evolving from the words,

> "There is still one thing that you lack. Sell all that you have and distribute to the poor, and you will have treasure in heaven. And come, follow me." (Lk 18:22)

How are we to follow Jesus into poverty and to the poor?

Jesus is inexhaustible; he will always be new, he will always be news. Jesus is so much that we can each make a new and original discovery of him for others and therein discover the secret treasure of our own heart. And this does not primarily pertain to theologians. It was the simple people, the little ones, who fascinated and astonished Jesus. And he in turn will be our eternal fascination and endless delight.

We will never exhaust Jesus and the Good News. We will never catch up with what he is. So, being Christian is always so much more ahead of us than behind us. The words of Jesus, like his person, have depths which we will never fully fathom. No logic, linguistics or hermeneutics will be sufficient. Those who *live* his truth will come to understand him. Jesus' words are like the koans of a Zen Master, pointing to a consciousness and a reality beyond the conceptual and verbal. When Jesus in John's gospel says, "You always have the poor with you," he may in some way be intimating his final promise in Matthew's gospel, that he will be with us always, even to the close of the age.

Is Jesus to be with us always as the poor? There is no choice more obvious, more deliberate, more consistent than Jesus' decision to be poor. He chooses to be poor in every critical moment of his life—his conception at Nazareth, his birth at Bethlehem, as a refugee family in Egypt, life with his disciples and companions, as a fugitive from the Pharisees with a price on his head, his cross, his death and burial. His teaching to the multitudes was a handing on of himself to the poor. His sacraments are poor, like water and desert bread. Without the poor, there can be no Christianity, no following of Jesus. Being poor is the first and the core of the Beatitudes, and the only beatitude in the present tense. "Blessed are the poor, for theirs IS the Kingdom of Heaven."

Yet, as Johannes Metz points out, "Poverty of Spirit is always betrayed most by those who are closest to it. It is the disciples of Christ in the Church who criticize and subvert it most savagely." A French agnostic cried in anguish, "We have had thirty-three years of Jesus and now nineteen hundred of betrayal." An American religious sister as she entered St.

Peter's in Rome, simply shook her head and said, "Poor Jesus!"

At the Last Supper, Jesus said to his disciples, "One of you is about to betray me *now*." Eventually, everyone did. And all of us in turn betray Him, the Gospel, individually and corporately. Yet, in Paul's words,

> "If we are faithless, he remains faithful—for He cannot deny himself." (2 Tim 2:13)

He continues to embarrass us by working through us, and through us, manifests Himself to the world.

Sometimes, in attempting to be faithful in little things, we come to betray the totality. This is religious poverty! Individual simplicity led to corporate affluence and isolation from the ordinary situation. Housekeepers, cooks, maintenance personnel were considered ordinary for people with a vow of poverty. How different from the poverty of those who work all day— and then have to work some more cleaning, cooking and taking care of the family and one another! It is a strange gospel poverty that disinvests itself from ghetto areas, that segregates people from dangerous or hard situations.

Sometimes when a gospel value is lost, submerged or underdeveloped, the Spirit has a way of embarrassing us in the Gospels to the wisdom of the contemporary generation. As in our Lord's day, "the children of this generation are constantly wiser than the children of light." Chesterton remarked that every heresy is the revenge of a forgotten truth, a revenge of something forgotten in the Gospel. Thus Marxism, in its way, proclaims the dignity of the good news to the poor and the oppressed, where those of us who have, turn our heads the other way.

This compels us to ponder the meaning of the parable of the talents:

> "For to everyone who has will be given more, and they will have more than enough; but from those who have not, even what they have will be taken away." (Mt 25:29)

We tend so often to see this "having" as material wealth or vocational gifts. Yet special "talents" are found with the poor—the gifts of faith, of perseverance and patience, of hope ... the gifts of the Spirit are theirs—and to them will be given even more!

The Gospel is a revolution, a revolution that makes all revolutions anemic by comparison. New light and energy are continually breaking through from the Gospels—like the light from stars which have never been seen before. We become responsible for this new light and energy that compels us to see our society's way of life in new perspectives. When we least expect it, Jesus interrupts our good life and cries out,

> "The time has come and the Kingdom of God is close at hand. Repent and believe the Good News." (Mk 1:15)

A most dangerous, yet most common, delusion is to believe that we are already Christian, that we are spiritual, that we have already arrived, that we no longer have to move. Jesus is always going on ahead; we will always be in exodus, on pilgrimage. To be Christian, to be on a spiritual journey, is to live in tents, to be always breaking camp, to move, to be going from one *metanoia* to another, from one conversion to another, from manna to manna, from Eucharist to Eucharist, from poor to poor. Discovering Jesus is to discover the poor. Union with Jesus is solidarity with the poor.

> "I tell you solemnly in so far as you neglected to do this to one of the least of these, you neglected to do it to Me." (Mt 25:45)

The holy question of our day is this: can anyone be truly human, can anyone be Christian, without identifying and living with the poor? The Catholic Worker movement, the Little Brothers and Sisters of Jesus, the Missionaries of Charity have discovered the ancient, yet always new depths of the Beatitudes through their relating to and living with the poor. In the fourth century, St. John Chrysostom recognized the poor as the ambassadors of Christ. Today we might well recognize the poor as our evangelists, the ones closest to the Gospel, as the ones who refuse to settle for anything less than Jesus.

In *Raids On the Unspeakable*, Thomas Merton says it well:

> "Into this world, this demented inn, in which there is absolutely no room for Him at all, Christ has come uninvited. But because He cannot be at home in it, because he is out of place in it, his place is with those others for whom there is no room. His place is with those who do not belong, who are rejected by power because they are regarded as weak, those who are discredited, who are denied the status of persons, who are tortured, bombed and exterminated. With those for whom there is no room, Christ is present in the world. He is mysteriously present in those for whom there seems to be nothing but the world at its worst."

Two capital sins of our culture are materialism and individualism. The more things we acquire, the more we are cut off from one another and the more fearful we become of each other. We become so poor that we have to buy everything. Yet the most important realities cannot be bought, collected or possessed by oneself. The deepest values are only experienced in sharing. There is but one path to Jesus and it is the same path which he took to come to us. He emptied himself of everything so that he could become one with us. He has told us where we can find him—in the sacrament of the poor. How really poor and simple are his words, his disciples, his remembrances. All that he left for us was bread to sustain our desert journey and wine for the dancing. Being poor does not necessarily lead to love, but love always leads to being poor. Blessed are those who love enough to be poor, who become free enough to be poor with the Poor One.

We can find no clearer or more specific source for how we as Christians are to live our lives than in the parables of Jesus. Yet all too frequently, most of us live them superficially. We can take, for example, the parable of the Good Samaritan (Lk 10:25-37), and through our imaginations come to see how far we have come, how far we have yet to go in identifying with Jesus:

Imagine yourself walking down the steep and desolate road from Jerusalem to Jericho—about 16 miles. You are all alone on this journey. It might be like walking in Central Park or in the inner city alone at night. Suddenly, you are attacked by several robbers. They beat you. They take everything you have. Then, they run off, leaving you barely conscious and bleeding.

How might it feel to suddenly become a victim?.... Where in your life have you felt like a victim?.... Try to imagine how the robbers feel. What do you think is missing in their lives that allows them to exploit others? ... Is there a robber in you? ... What have you robbed from others—their freedom? their job? their dignity?.... Withholding is another way we rob others, ourselves, God.... Where do you find yourself limiting your time ... your talents ... your love?

Come back now to the Jericho road. Imagine that you are the priest going down the same road—perhaps on the way to the Temple. How do you feel when you encounter the beaten, needy one lying in the ditch? Does your heart connect momentarily? Do you offer a silent prayer—for someone else to help, someone who is not already about God's work? By touching this one you would become unclean for days, unable to perform your priestly duties— and you believe the Law must be followed beyond anything else. So you quickly pass to the other side of the road.

Can you identify with the priest in you? Are there situations, people, issues you would prefer to pass by rather than to risk getting involved, rather than to risk what others might say of you? How often do you get caught by the letter of the law to the deadening of the spirit of the law? Are there times that you are rigid rather than thoughtfully flexible?

Suppose that you are that Levite passing along this same road. You are in a hurry. As a protector of the rules and laws of society, you are a good and upright citizen. You have appointments to keep, committee meetings, speaking

7

Free to Plunge into the Incarnation

What is your experience of the mystery of the Incarnation? How often great truths are given to us long before we can understand them and live them consciously. Great truths of the faith, handed down from generation to generation, remain for the most part so hidden, so un-understood, that when in a special moment a radiance breaks through, we are startled and overwhelmed. So, startle us, Lord! Overwhelm us! In our day, we are ready for a new breakthrough of Incarnation.

What does Incarnation do to you and to me? What happens when divine awareness breaks into human consciousness? What is the mystery of Jesus' thirty years of Nazareth? The Incarnation is cumulative. The Word of God increases generation upon generation. What will happen in our day as human consciousness reaches a limit and saturation point that almost blows the circuit? Are you ready?

In recent years the "black holes" of outer space have become a fascinating phenomenon for study. They have created a crisis, perhaps the priority crisis in astro-physics. What happens in the death of a giant star, in a catastrophic gravitational collapse? Matter crushes together with such enormous force that it literally compresses itself out of existence. Can you imagine the earth compressing itself into the size of a quarter-inch ball bearing? And then further, until it compresses itself out of existence? The star becomes a singularity. Its matter is squeezed into an infinitesimally small volume; it becomes infinitely dense with an infinitely high gravitational force so great that it prevents the escape of light! Imagine, a gravitational force so immense that not even light can escape from it! This is why a black hole in outer space is invisible, unable to be seen by any kind of scientific apparatus. Yet scientific data compels us to believe in the presence of such an incredible phenomenon.

Another hypothesis beyond the wildest scientific fiction is that of a "white hole", a hypothetical point in space from which energy and matter are poured into the universe. The black holes in outer space are like vacuum cleaners in the universe. They draw immense matter into them and it disappears. One theory holds that in another universe somewhere else, through some kind of a subterranean underground this matter reappears through a "white hole". Although there is considerable scientific evidence for the black holes in outer space, "white holes" exist only as hypothesis for now. Yet these images of modern science, along with the new expanding universe of the human mind, give us new language, new metaphors to begin to understand in another dimension something of what Incarnation is.

Could it not be that Incarnation is the "white hole" that scientists are looking for? Could it not be that there has been an immense amount of new energy and of light poured into the world? A recent theory of a new form of entropy ties in strikingly with this. The third law of thermodynamics holds that everything runs out of energy, slows down and eventually dies. Every star runs out of energy. In the Christian era, there seems to be a contradiction of the law of entropy, a kind of reverse entropy. Sometime two thousand years ago, entropy as we know it reversed itself. Ever since the birth of Christ a new kind of energy, a new kind of depth and richness seems to be radiating into our universe. An apparent scientific verification of this occurred in a small village in northern Israel around 752 Roman Era (4 B.C.), when an immense amount of energy was released. And this energy, this life has continued to increase. Again and again, it breaks through in very unexpected ways, especially in times of great catastrophic diminishment.

As never before, we can begin to think of Incarnation with

language and metaphors that did not exist before. A call to wholeness is coming out of catastrophe. Nothing exists in isolation. There is always a balance, a tension. We are caught today between wholeness and disintegration, between wholeness and brokenness, wholeness and emptiness. Incarnation is a call to wholeness, to holiness, to oneness, to universality in its root meaning—being catholic.

What is the totality of Jesus' Incarnation? He became everything that we are, except in sin, in order to draw us into everything that He is. He did not simply become human; He brought a whole new depth and height and breadth to what being human is. Our call is to become as human as Jesus is—a humanist that we can only call divine. Nothing human is unknown to Him, yet how much that is human was hidden from us until Christ became what we are. He cannot take just a little of us. He tabernacles in us. He pitches His tent among us, in us, and He opens a new universe.

Most of us are like the black holes in outer space. We have so absorbed the tremendous, unimaginable energy and power and life of Incarnation; yet, there is such a bottomless depth in us that no light, or very little light, has escaped from us. The ancient and contemporary world continues to indict us with their word, "I see no difference." The Word became flesh, and it doesn't seem to make much difference.

What is the human awareness of the divine inbreaking, that

> "that life was the light of men, a light that shines in the dark, a light that darkness could not overpower.... He was in the world that had its being through Him and the world did not know Him." (Jn 1)

What is the divine awareness of the human mystery? The Word becoming flesh has made the human mysterious, has given the human length and breadth, and height and depth that it never had in itself. The divine has stretched the human. Incarnation is the Word about who God is; and, we are each a word of God. Within each one of us dwells the creative Spirit, dwells the energy of divine Love. We carry it in our genes. How can we be free enough to allow that Spirit to transform us and the world?

Incarnation is open to us; Christ is alive in His body—the Church. Christ comes alive in us as we become free enough to give Him our heart; and then, we begin to recognize the One who is the Heart of our heart. Every time we act in such a way as to reveal God, every time we abandon ourselves into God's hands, we participate in Incarnation. Each time we celebrate the liturgy, the sacraments of the Church, we live the mystery of the Incarnation. And as we witness to Christ's life in us, we can feel ourselves to be one corpuscle in His blood, one cell in His body. How can He live without us?

And living through the commemoration of Jesus' life, we are born into the mystery of His life in us. How do you give birth to Christ? How do you act as midwife to His birth in others? Do you nurture Him as the child within you, care for Him as the child in others? Do you allow Him to discipline you, to help you to grow? How do you assist or abet His growth in your family, your friends, your enemies? Have you spent lonely days in the desert with Him struggling to resist temptation? Are you an angel feeding Him in your neighbor? Have you allowed Satan to speak through you to separate another from Him? How do you carry His cross? Are you free enough to be vulnerable to another helping you shoulder your cross? Who have you nailed to the Cross? Can you sit with the women at the Cross and wait, with the women at the tomb and wait for Resurrection? Are you at home when the Spirit breathes a word in you? Who will you follow? Are you free to plunge into the Incarnation? How do you live the mysteries of Incarnation from Christmas to Easter, from Easter to Pentecost?

Has it been necessary for the work of the scientific endeavors to stretch the minds and hearts of men and women to begin to have the capacity for Incarnation? To develop the wonder, the awe that

> " Through Him all things came to be. Not one thing had its being but through Him. All that came to be has life in Him, and that life is the light of men and women."

(Jn 1:3-4)

What kind of consciousness happens in us because the divine

has broken through and has drawn us out of the bottomless pit into the "white hole" of revelation?

"But to all who do accept Him, He gives power to become children of God; to all who believe in the name of Him, He lives among us and we see His glory, His presence transparent. Indeed from His fullness, from His wholeness we have all of us received. Yes, transparency in return for transparency, light for light. No one has ever seen God. It is the only Son who is nearest to the Father's heart who has made Him known." (cf. Jn 1:12-18)

And who continues to make Him known. What is this power, this mysterious energy and force that happens in us? How free are we to recognize it, to abandon ourselves to it?

I have often been asked about reincarnation, so fascinating to the contemporary mind. And I have responded, "Yes, I believe in reincarnation." I tell them I am an Incarnation. That I believe that I have been seized and caught, that I live a life that is beyond myself. There is a life in me that I can never adequately touch. There is an understanding and a consciousness, a prayer and a love deeper than myself and I do not know where it comes from. There is a new consciousness that is beyond anything that has ever been dreamed or touched by the human alone.

Do we dare to believe that we are Incarnation, that He has touched into each of our lives? We call it a baptism, that we have plunged into Father, Son and Holy Spirit. We have been invaded by extra-terrestrial life. The divinity becomes human and the human is taken up into divinity.

The mystery of Jesus' wholeness is emptiness, is *kenosis*. He emptied. He was free to be poor, to empty Himself out so totally He could enter into our brokenness. He became everything that we are. There is nothing human except sin that is unknown to Him. Everything human now has a new depth and a new expansion. Literally, the new creation is far more astonishing than the original creation, and yet it is hidden. The Incarnation continues to increase in every generation, and yet it will always remain hidden. It can never be touched except through faith. Not because it is not real, but because it is more real than the physical. In some ways it demands more faith, not less faith. Not only did He become human, not only did He come down to our level, it would have been enough that the divinity became human. But He stepped even below our level; incredible as it may seem, He became our food and drink.

The ultimate validation and evidence of Incarnation is Eucharist. A whole new depth of self-awareness and a wholeness of integration happens because He became bread to be broken and wine to be spilled, that He took up into Himself even our food. And this cannot be touched except in contemplation, in prayer. There is a new depth in the human person that can only be discovered together, only in church, in community, in assembly through interlocking energies. By ourselves we always forget. Only through one another can we be compelled to live beyond ourselves.

Ultimate truth is communicated and received only through individuals being in touch with other individuals. We cannot know ourselves by ourselves; we cannot save ourselves by ourselves. We are a collage of our families, friends, enemies, lovers, children, community, country, our place in history. By this we are called to be unique, whole individuals, incarnations of God's word and love for others, in others. We are each called to be an individual consciousness, an indivisible unity, a unique, singular person related as much to others as to ourselves. To be incarnate is to be in the body. How many of us are really at home in our bodies? How many are often "out for lunch?" Only when we are free enough to *be* who we truly are, are we free to create genuine community with others, free to *be* there with and for others building relationship, free to value the uniqueness of another, free to plunge into the Incarnation.

What was the mystery of Jesus in His human consciousness discovering who He was? How long did it take for Jesus to come to understand that He was the Son of God? Do we dare to believe the truth: that if God continues to enter our life, we become His body, His blood, and His Resurrection; that we have an identity beyond our psychological identity; that we have an identity in sacrament, in His mystery? Are we yet capable of such truth? The truth of ourselves, the truth of Himself? The more we come to self-awareness, the more we become aware of our brokenness, the more we become aware of our need to be redeemed, to be freed, to be saved. He became our brokenness so that we can become whole, so that we can answer the call to wholeness in the body of Christ.

What was Jesus' self-awareness of Himself as human? What was Jesus' awareness of Himself as being the Son of God? Of being universal brother? What happened in Jesus that He was compelled to identify with everyone, especially the least? What compelled Him to choose the marginal, the poor, and the broken, the ones who no one else had any time for? What was Jesus' self-awareness in His identity with the poor? Why did He call them the privileged members of His Kingdom? "If you but knew the gift of God."

Why did Paul in his great letter to the Ephesians cry out so often and with such startling awareness,

> "Before the world was made, He chose us; He chose us in Christ to be holy and spotless, to be holy (and transparent, freed from ourselves, freed from selfishness, freed from isolation), to live through love in His presence. Determined that we should become His adopted sons and daughters through Christ Jesus in whom through His blood we gain our freedom, the forgiveness of our sins. He has let us know the mystery of His purpose, His hidden plan." (Eph 1:4-9)

Never before in human history have we come so close to a cosmic despair. We cannot hold it together. Yet, how simple are Paul's words to us as he continues,

> "... the hidden plan He so kindly made in Christ from the beginning to act upon when the times had run their course to the end. That He would bring everything together under Christ, as head. Everything in the heavens, in the cosmos, in the universe, everything on earth. And it is in Him that we were claimed as God's own, chosen from the beginning. Now you too in Him have heard the message of the truth and the Good News of your liberation and have believed it,

(or have you?). And you too have been stamped with the
seal of the Holy Spirit of the promise, the wholeness of our
inheritance,   which brings freedom for those whom God
has taken for His own—to make His presence transparent."
(Eph 1:9-14)

For the hidden Jesus, so hidden in us that we are the "black
holes" of our cosmos, is the anonymous Jesus. How long will
it take to come to the wholeness of self-awareness, the awareness of faith? "I know Him in whom I believe." How long will
it take to see, to have His vision?

The word of God is an invitation to explore. Like prayer,
we are always losing it. But it can never really be lost. It haunts
us, it clings to us, it finds us again and again. In Christ there is
always new creation. There is always new bread, new consciousness, new awareness. Again and again He comes; two
thousand years are but as a day. He comes as our daily bread,
our daily surprise, our daily wonder—a new awareness, a new
vision, a new faith.

With the Incarnation, a totally new joy poured into the
world. This joy is first of all a gift, a gift which is unique to
Christianity, a distinctive sign of the overflowing of the Holy
Spirit. All of creation disposes the mind and the heart of the
human person to meet joy, the joy that one experiences when
one is with nature. But the deepest human joy is always to be
found in sharing and in communion with other people. Yet
human joy is always fragile, always incomplete; it is so easily
threatened. Technological society has succeeded in multiply-
ing the opportunities for pleasure, but it has great difficulty in
generating joy because joy of its very essence is spiritual. It
comes from another source, a much deeper source.

Every sacrament, every sacramental provides an environment for us to experience joy. Celebration, festival, feast is to
experience a transcendence even in the presence of suffering.
When there is no reason to celebrate, the Christian celebrates!
The ultimate protest against oppression is a fiesta!

In essence, Christian joy is a spiritual sharing in the unfathomable joy, both divine and human, which is in the heart of Jesus
Christ. Is there anyone who can enjoy himself (or herself)

more than that person who is in Christ? The most constant tradition which we have as Christians is that a Christian is one who is an alleluia from head to toe. Not a passing joy, but a joy which is continually unfolding, being discovered. The joy of the Christian is something which increases throughout history. There is more joy today than ever before in the millenniums of human existence. That joy is the promise of Jesus; it is the mustard seed growing and expanding.

The Incarnation invites us to discover that joy is the good news, that He has come that we may have life and joy more abundantly. Giving in a burst of joyful generosity and joyful gratitude is at the heart of the Christian message—"so that the love with which you love me may be in them, so that I may be in them." This kind of joy is a demanding joy, a joy which no one can take from us. One of the most astonishing promises that Jesus made is that "Joy may be in you, and that in you it may reach its fullness." We all love to see a person who can really enjoy himself or herself. How much must be God's enjoyment of Himself! What must be our enjoyment of God's enjoyment of ourselves!

" Happy are those who carry the good news." This is not a beatitude, a blessing, in isolation. Its meaning is seen only in the whole context of the strange kinds of blessings which seem so paradoxical and contradictory.

> "Happy are you when people abuse you and persecute you and speak all kinds of calumny against you on my account. Happy are you. Rejoice and be glad for your reward will be great in heaven. This is how they persecuted the prophets before you." (Mt 5:11-12)

What is the sadness of the unbelievers of our time? There is a cumulative Christian joy; yet, at the same time, there is a diminishment of human possibility with the sadness of those who cannot believe. Never before has there been such a psychic inability to believe the good news and to accept the Spirit of God. The first fruits of Christian joy are Eucharist, community. The Eucharist is essentially the celebration of the joy of His presence in each other—"for the sake of that joy, which was still in the future, He endured the cross." Christian joy cannot exist of itself. This joy can happen only out of the crucible, the mystery of the cross, which leads to an incomprehensible kind of joy, the joy that is evident in little children. One of the most beautiful passages of Paul's letter on Christian joy speaks of the Church as the true youth of the world, of her secret of permanent youth being generated by the Holy Spirit. With Jesus' coming, He brought all newness and joy by bringing His own person; with His coming, He brought an invitation to each of us to journey to the inner place where the Father, Son and Holy Spirit welcome us into their own intimacy in Divine unity.

Each of us is a fragment of His self-awareness—the dream of the Father and of the Son. Julian of Norwich says it well:

> "We are 'knit into' God because He was 'oned' with our flesh."

When do we become the child of our Father? How long will it take to dream the dream of our Father? How long to discover the mystery hidden in the dream of the Father and the Son? The mystery hidden unto our day, but perhaps opened up to us as never before because we are children of this generation, and the next generation will be wiser than we are.

Am I changed by my vision, by my faith? I change and enter a new level of presence when I dare to believe, to dream. I am transformed by my concept of myself, my self-perception, my self-prophecy. I am transformed by my reach. The vision is within ourselves, and yet never before have we experienced a vision and a reach so far beyond ourselves.

Human vision is inexhaustible since Christ now becomes the measure of what is human. The human has become the means of being divine, of being as human as Jesus is. We are the image of God in our capacity for self-awareness. What must be the enjoyment God has of Himself? What joy we are called into because we are that image. Imagine the dream the Father has for each of us. A dream so real that it becomes creation, a love so immense that it becomes Incarnation, divinization. Imagine Jesus' love and what He sees in each of us, that He could dream we could be like Himself. We are the image of God in our capacity for self-awareness, for being dreamers and co-dreamers. We dream together in Him because He pours a life into us that is His life becoming our life, our deepest self.

In the self-awareness of Jesus is the mystery of Eucharist.

> "Take and eat. This is my body given for you; this is my blood to be shed for you." (cf. Lk 22: 19-20)

What is Eucharist? What is He doing in this Eucharist? The Eucharist is His gift to us of ourselves. In giving us Himself, He gives us the deepest gift of ourselves. In giving us Himself, He gives us the gift of one another, the gift of everyone.

To be free to plunge into Incarnation, anyone who brings his or her gift to the altar and recalls that his brother or sister has anything against them, leaves the gift and goes to be reconciled. The self-awareness of Jesus is to light a fire on earth and He wishes that blaze were ignited now. If our world is dark, if our city has no hope, then it is because we who have been given the light, the self-awareness, the faith, have believed more in the power of darkness than in the power of Jesus, than in the power of love. We will be free for Incarnation when we choose to let go of ourselves and take on the wholeness of the body of Christ. The self-awareness of Jesus is real. "I live now not I, but He lives in me." If only we could believe it. We are the ones who must cry out, "Lord, that I may see."

> "If your eye, the vision, is not functioning, your whole body will be in darkness. If the light of self-awareness inside you is darkness, what darkness that will be." (Lk 11:33-35)

Jesus is still the light of the world. There will be no human development that will ever come close to the light of Jesus.

"Those who believe in me will never walk in darkness." He proclaims not only that He is the light of the world, but that we, you and I, are the light of the world. The self-awareness of Jesus, in its fullest expression, is to echo the seventeenth chapter of John's gospel. Eternal life is this, "to know you, the only true God, and Jesus Christ whom you have sent." I have made your Kingdom and your vision, your home known to the men and women you took from the world to give me. And he concludes with that great prayer,

> "I have made your name known. I have made your kingdom known to them and will continue to make it known so the love with which you loved me may be in them, and so that I may be in them." (Jn 17:6,26)

Perhaps it is only the saints and the poets who understand. T.S. Eliot expressed it as only a poet could:

> "But to apprehend the point of intersection of the timeless with time, is an occupation for the saint—no occupation either, but something given and taken, in a lifetime's death in love, ardour and selflessness and self-surrender. For most of us, there is only the unattended moment, the moment in and out of time, the distraction fit, lost in a shaft of sunlight, the wild thyme unseen, or the winter lightning or the waterfall, or music heard so deeply that it is not heard at all, but you are the music while the music lasts. These are only hints and guesses, hints followed by guesses; and the rest is prayer, observance, discipline, thought and action. The hint half guessed, the gift half understood, is Incarnation."

God becoming human; the divine awareness lifting up human consciousness.

And our faith is the awareness of Jesus become human, more human than any of us will ever dare to be, uttering His word to us and in us, daring us to follow, to believe the truth. If we could only follow; if we could only believe the truth that we are in Him, and He is in us. All that He has learned from the Father, He has given to us and so He dares to call us His friends.

> "As the Father has loved me, I love you.
> As the Father sends me, I send you."

And Jesus, day in and day out, continues to utter His self-awareness, His wholeness for our brokenness until we someday will be able to say, "It is the Lord," and He will say in return, "Yes, it is Myself." And then we shall be free.

When we are free to plunge into the Incarnation, to live "not as I live, but as Christ lives in me," we are free to be holy. More and more, our lives move toward the creation of the kingdom here on earth, our everyday acts become sanctified, and we become a gift to the glory of God.

8

Free to Live the Call of Holiness

The call of holiness is a call into the cloud of unknowing. The call to be holy is a call into the inner-most depths, to the inward center—the stillpoint. Holiness calls us to be humble before God. Am I holy? Am I beginning to be holy? Take a few minutes to become aware of the silence within yourself.... Now, try to call to mind your experience of the holy—the words of God that have in some way touched you.

"God has saved us and called us to a holy life, not because of any merit of ours, but according to his own design, the grace held out to us in Christ Jesus before the world began." (2 Tm 1:9)

"God chose us before the world began to be holy and blameless in his sight—to be full of love." (Eph 1:4)

"Become holy yourselves in every aspect of your lives, after the likeness of the Holy One who called you." (1 Pet 1:15)

"Be holy, for I am holy." (Lev 19:2)

"We are invited to serve him devoutly without fear through all our days, to be holy in his sight." (Lk 1:74-75)

"Put on the new person created in God, in God's image, whose justice and holiness are born of truth." (Eph 4:24)

"If anyone destroys God's temple, God will destroy that

one. For the temple of God is holy and you are that temple."
(1 Cor 3:17)

"May the Lord strengthen your hearts, making them
blameless and holy before our God and Father, at the
coming of our Lord Jesus with all his holy ones." (1 Thess
3:13)

"Strive for peace with all people, and for the holiness
without which no one will see the Lord." (Heb 12:14)

What is your experience of the call to holiness? How are you
holy?

Kadosh, Kadosh, Kadosh ... Hagias, Hagias, Hagias ...
Sanctus, Sanctus, Sanctus ... Holy, Holy, Holy—in Hebrew,
Greek, Latin, English—still the mystery remains. And part of
the mystery is that we think we are the ones pursuing God.
What a surprise to discover that it is God who, all the time,
has been in pursuit of us! There is something in each one of us
that God loves that we do not know! May the Spirit enable us
to discover that hidden self, that hidden power, that hidden
gift.

Reflecting on this call to holiness, I am reminded of a contemporary writer, Lewis Thomas, who is an agnostic and one of
the finest essay writers in science today. In his best seller,
Medusa and the Snail, he writes,

> "The only solid piece of scientific truth about which I feel
> confident is that we are profoundly ignorant about nature.
> Indeed I regard this as the major discovery of the past
> hundred years of biology. It is in its way an illuminating
> piece of news. It would have amazed the brightest minds of
> the 18th century enlightenment to be told by any of us how
> little we know, and how bewildering seems the way ahead.
> It is this sudden confrontation with the depth and scope of
> ignorance that represents the most significant contribution
> of 20th century science to the human intellect."

The most significant contribution of 20th-century science to
the human intellect is the depth and scope of our ignorance! I

think we could say that today about our theology. It is a learned ignorance, and perhaps in no area are we more unlearned, ignorant, than in the realm of the holy.

Lewis Thomas went on to say,

> "There is nothing at all absurd about the human condition. We matter. It seems to me a good guess hazarded by a good many people who have thought of it, that we may be engaged in the formation of something like a mind for the life of this planet. If this is so, we are still at the most primitive stage, still stumbling with language and thinking, but infinitely capacitated for the future. Looked at this way, it is remarkable that we have come as far as we have in so short a period—really, no time at all. As geologists measure time, we are the newest, the youngest, and the brightest beings around."

"We may be engaged in the formation of something like a mind for the life of this planet." And could we not say that we, as the people of God, as the Body of Christ, are involved in something like the formation of a spirit, or a soul, for the culture of the 21st century. How imperative that we find a soul and a spirit for technology and the computerized world! Never before have we been more dangerous to the ongoing reality of our history.

Lewis Thomas says optimistically, "We are infinitely capacitated for the future." How truly Jesus' disciples, called to be holy, can deeply affirm and recognize that "we are infinitely capacitated for the future." We are "the newest, the youngest, the brightest beings around." Those who respond to the call of holiness have always been the prophetic element in the church, the cutting edge. How sad it will be if we do not continue that heritage. Yet, whether we do or not, that spirit is at work.

Kadosh, Hagias, Sanctus, Holy—in every liturgy there is that great pause as we enter the Eucharistic prayer where we are reminded of the ancient tradition of Moses, Isaiah, of all the prophets—that God is other, totally other, infinitely transcendent. The word "holy" belongs to God alone. Holy—a word that has no definition, no description. When Karl Barth attempted to describe the holy, he asked,"Is it the man (or woman) who trembles before God?" And he bewailed the fact that there are so few who tremble before God. Who is the person of our century who has the capacity to tremble before God?

A great Russian novelist of the nineteenth century mourned the fact that there were so few who could feel the anguish of not being able to pray. What a loss—the incapacity to experience the anguish of not being able to pray! That was a hundred years ago. Where are we today?

How strange is that word, *holy*. Even we who are committed to that journey, how rarely, how rarely do we let ourselves experience something of that trembling. "Take off your shoes, you are on holy ground!" Prostrate yourself, climb the mountain, fast for forty days so you can open yourself to the fire and the cloud, the wind, the energy, the violence of God. God is violent. Will it take a Mt. St. Helens in our backyard to recognize that God is still God? The God of world religions is the God that all of us are ready to meet. We can experience the tremor, we can experience the awe, and in certain moments, we each have been touched by that holiness.

The God of Christian holiness is different and evokes a special kind of holiness. Yet, if we do not know the Kadosh of the past, then we will not be ready for the Sanctus of the present. How unique Christian holiness is—the call of the Incarnation, of the Resurrection, of the Eucharist. We are always ready for the God of violence and of power, but will we ever be ready for the God who is poor, the God who is powerless? Can we bear to attempt to comprehend the Abba of Jesus, who so loved His son, and so poured Himself out into His son, that if it were possible there would be nothing left of Him. The God who empties Himself out is the God who has so much power that He can become almost nothing. The *kenosis*, the emptying out. The call of Jesus, the call of Christian holiness is the call to become as human as Jesus—to become as real, to become as whole, to become as intimate as Jesus. Christian holiness demands infinite power because it can only be lived in total emptying.

One of Mother Teresa's sisters once said that her secret gift is that she is free to be nothing and, therefore, God can use her for anything. The call to holiness is the call to be free to be nothing, free to be poor so that God can use us for anything. That call is not a simple call, for at every moment a multiplicity of calls impinge and break into our mind and body's space. The tension to be me, to be other, to be fulfilled, to be emptied—the call by the world, the call by history, the call of the 20th-century culture and, at the same time, the call of our roots, of our traditions, of the future.

Who is it that calls? Is it a call of my own being? Is it a call beyond myself? Is it a call to happiness? Is it a call to creativity? One young woman responded to my question, "How do you experience the call to holiness?" with the words, "It is not a call to happiness. The call to happiness, the call to save one's soul can be the narrowest form of selfishness. It is something more."

Christian holiness is still awesome. It is as awkward and as embarrassing as Jesus' question, "Who do you say I am?" In telling Jesus who He is, we reveal who we are. "Where I am, I want you to be." Where shall we find Him? Where did Paul find Him? "Who I am, I want you to become."

When Jesus asked, "Who do you say I am?" Peter answered, "You are the Messiah, the chosen one of God." Jesus accepted Peter at that moment, where he was. Jesus' own name for Himself was, "Son of Man"—simply, "I am human." Jesus is the one who is most human. "If you want to be my disciple, deny your very self. Take up your cross and come, follow me."

The call to holiness is a call to heroism, to self-sacrifice, to totality, to emptiness, to be poor. The call to be holy demands a silence, a stillness, and a listening. One cannot hear the gospel unless one *needs* to hear the good news. Perhaps it is only the poor who can hear the gospel. The poor are the closest to God because they are the most powerless. Jesus was compelled to gravitate to the poor because the poor are most like God. They are powerless; they are almost nothing. That is the holiness of Jesus.

A Baptist minister described the need to learn the three R's, if we are to follow Jesus today: relocation, redistribution and reconciliation. To relocate ourselves we must move, we must change, we must be converted, not necessarily in space, but certainly in our way of being in the world. We must be prepared to take the Abrahamic journey, the Mosaic journey, the journey of Jesus from Nazareth to Jerusalem—the journey of the church from Jerusalem to Rome and wherever we are called to journey today.

Redistribution, like the law of holiness, parallels the call of the Eucharist: to be taken, to be blessed, to be broken, to be handed out. We are called by the world, the Third World. We are called by the poor. We are called by the world, the flesh, and the devil. We are tugged at by our cultural milieu. We are drawn, attracted, inspired and kindled. We are called to prayer; we are called to affluence. We are called to achievement; we are called to penance. We are called to protest; we are called to prophetic action. And perhaps most of all, we are called to one another. Gandhi reminds us, "If you can't find God in the very next person you meet, it is a waste of time to look further." And, if we cannot be reconciled with those closest to us, it is futile to think we can be instruments of peace in the world.

One consequence of the Eucharist is to bring people together to do the work of God. The harvest of the Eucharist is the revelation, the recognition of what God is doing in our midst, within us and between us. It is the call to the city and the call to the desert. How do you experience the call of holiness? What do you expect of yourself? What do you expect of life? Of God? What do you expect of the Church? What does it profit to gain the whole world? What dream would you like to make come true in your life? What prophecy are you making of yourself? Are you infinitely capacitated for the future? Together we are in the process of the formation of making something like a soul and a spirit for the contemporary world. We are called, we are led, we are driven. We are called to follow, to be present, to be given, to be expanded. We are called by the gospel. The danger and power of the gospel is that someone always listens, an immense power is released, and we are never the same again.

A holy person experiences things differently. Every thing, every relationship is changed. We are called to create, to build, to lay the imprint of the image of God on all things—to

restore and recreate all things in His image. We are haunted
by God. Dorothy Day described this as a "harsh and dreadful
love." T.S. Eliot in *Little Gidding* says of holiness, it is "a
condition of complete simplicity costing not less than everything." The gospel can be harsh and dreadful; yet, at the same
time, it is gentle and tender. Do you experience the *temptation*
of holiness? Intuitively, all of us know the danger. Of all things,
be most careful of love, of holiness. Yet, we are called to be a
communion of saints, communities of holy people.

We are called to love, and to service and to fidelity. There is
only one sign of love and that is fidelity. Anyone can love for a
moment, for a year, but only His spirit enables us to be faithful
to the end. Each of us can make our own litany of the call, of
the imperatives of Jesus, of the call to life—life most abundantly. We are called in a new way to be catholic. We are
almost embarrassed with that term today. We do not like to
be called catholic, to be universal brothers and sisters. That is
at the heart of the call to holiness—to be universal brothers
and sisters.

Holiness, if it is holiness, is always new. There is a new
holiness to our time because there are new situations, new
realities, new relationships. Holiness is always new as it is
always ancient. Holiness is a transcendence, a call to extrava-
gance, and perhaps even a call to what the world would call
wastefulness, that alabaster jar. For whom will you pour out
your alabaster jar? Upon whom will you waste your love? For
whom will you waste your life—as He wasted His life, His
love, for us? St. John of the Cross describes this freedom to
love, to be holy:

> "Anyone that with pure love works for God, not only
> cares not whether or not others know it, but does not even
> do these things so that God may know it. Such a person,
> even though it should never be known, would not cease to
> perform these same services and with the same gladness and
> love."

The call to holiness is a continuum, a spectrum from myself
to the mystics, the martyrs, the confessors, the fathers and

mothers of the church, the contemplatives. We are all called to be holy. There is no way of being human except to be holy, to be whole, to use all of one's talents. To whom much is given, much is expected. Yet each one is holy in his or her own way. No saint has ever been a saint by imitating another saint. Kadosh, Hagias, Sanctus, Holy . . . holiness is itself a passion calling each of us to live up to the limits of our potential. Leon Bloy wisely stated, "There is only one sadness, the sadness of not being a saint."

There is a saint, a holiness in each of us and the greatest journey is to discover that saint, that holiness within. In each of us is embodied one of the fragments of Jesus; and, Jesus is dependent upon each of us to be an unwritten gospel. The prophet, the holy person, is the one who experiences within him or herself a presence that is so rich and meaningful that they are compelled to share it with others. The holy person, who receives the gift of himself or herself, becomes almost intoxicated with the truth that everyone carries that hidden mystery.

The call of our day is to a higher consciousness, to respond to the work of God's love in us, not only in prayer, but in the kind of presence that we offer to our world and to our time, to the second creation that is always going on in us, to the inner evolution and revolution, to "the mystery at work in us," to the opening consecration. Perhaps today we can use an old word that has been practically forgotten—*transubstantiation.* There is something happening in us that is reflected each day in Eucharist. In the smallest particle of matter, how insignificant is the particle of bread that is changed into the presence of the risen Christ. Yet that is the mirror of what is happening in us.

The mystery of Christian holiness is the truth of the infinitesimally small, the poorness of the infinitesimally small, the almost nothing. Christian holiness is doing what God is doing— almost nothing. But we of this generation so easily get caught with what someone has called the "suppression of the sublime," the Jonah complex—the fear of our own greatness. The most subtle temptation of good people, who are really holy people, is the fear of one's own holiness and goodness. We flee from what He could do in us. We want to avoid knowledge, responsibility. Sometimes, too, we do not feel the anguish of not being able to pray.

Holy is still an awesome word. No one dares to take this title to him or herself. The holy is always hidden, most of all from the holy person. The moment you think yourself holy, you have lost it! In the monastic tradition, there is always a holy person in every community. One sign of the holy person is that he or she thinks everyone else is the saint of the community.

The Spirit is bringing something new into our midst. There is an intensification of faith and hope and love. There has been a cumulative deposit. Imagine 2,000 years of Incarnation! Imagine the cumulative deposit of wisdom, of prayer, of grace, of work. What an awesome tradition that is! Imagine the power that is there. In trying to uncover the sources of consciousness, research scientists use a new word—*bioluminescence*. At a certain level, life becomes so intense that it becomes incandescent. That is a wonderful word! The cumulative effect of God's word and sacrament in us makes us almost incandescent. Every once in a while we see the hidden halo, the bioluminescence of another. Imagine the energy and light that we carry within ourself, because God's invitation is that we become the burning bush, that we become the mountain, that we become the hearth, that we become the well with water leaping up to everlasting life, that we become the radiant presence of Jesus.

Holiness is the most basic truth of the Incarnation, of the Resurrection, of the Eucharist. There is a special kind of strength that comes from the struggle. One can never reach a mountaintop by looking at it. One does not have the energy. Only by climbing do we discover our inner power. Christian holiness is always hidden, always ordinary. The holy is as plain, as simple and as mysterious as the Eucharist: the ordinary holiness and goodness of elderly people, of young married couples, of workers—simple, everyday wholesomeness, warmth and love. Most of us know holiness in its mixed forms of the sinner-saint or the near saint, and not so much the canonized, the blessed or the venerable saint. We all know ourselves best, perhaps, as lapsed saints. Mostly, we are the Nazareth saints, the valley saints. Most of us are pilgrims who have seen the holiness of a long life of ordinariness, the holiness of inconsequentialness.

I asked a retired priest what his call to holiness had been. He had almost nothing to say, yet what he said is so much more than I could ever say. He answered, "The call to holiness is to love God more. The world is under God's direction and will continue to be."

I asked him what was most helpful to the people he served. He said, "What your life is, that you are doing your work, and that you care for your people. What helped most was seeing how good people are doing God's work." We are meant to be transformed into holiness through our daily lives. Everything is an opportunity for holiness; therefore, we are always winners! The call is to be Eucharist, to allow God to take us, to embrace us, to bless us and to pour Spirit into us. Only then can we be broken and passed around. Only when it is impossible for us to take the next step, can we begin the second journey—the journey that is taken within.

Some are born saints, some seem to achieve holiness, but most of us have holiness thrust upon us. Most of us are reluctantly and hesitantly holy. You are holy. Otherwise, you would not be reading this book, you would not be looking, you would not be searching. Each one of us knows our secret. No one but I know the grace I have never used, the journey I have never walked, the path never taken, the person never responded to. The gift has already been given. God alone is holy. You are the beloved, the chosen ones. The work of God is your holiness.

We have fear of the holy because we fear ourselves. We have fear of our own greatness. There is a new holiness—a holiness that is sanity in the midst of madness. "If we can only cope with life," someone told me, "that would be holiness." Holiness will do more than enable us to survive; already it is enabling so many in our time, our contemporaries, to be martyrs. Holiness, hidden and concealed, happens in the heart. I have a suspicion that there is a conspiracy to make each one of us holy. A bioluminescence is at work in each of us—the power of the infinitesimally small, the simplest prayer. Holiness is more comprehensive than prayer, sacraments, ministry or even the church. God had his son, Jesus. Jesus has us, his brothers and sisters, his friends. They breathe their love and their Spirit into us so that we can breathe it into the world and into one another. To grow in holiness means we must grow ever more deeply into communion with others, to companion one another on the way.

The call to holiness is at the deepest part of our being. All of us know it because we know from the Spirit. "God is in us, God is with us." The Beloved takes each of us and blesses us, embraces us, breathes Spirit into us. Only then does God break us, break our hearts, so that we can be free of ourselves to make room for someone else, to make room for the Spirit and all those we meet along life's path. The call to holiness is a call to emptiness, a call to be nothing, to be poor, to be so free God can use us for anything. Holiness calls us to

> "Let this mind be in you which was also in Christ Jesus who, though he was God, did not cling on to his equality with God, but emptied himself and took upon himself the form of a servant." (Phil 2:5-7)

It is a call to be broken and to be healed, to the wholeness of community, to oneness, to mystical union with God through Word and Eucharist. Holiness calls us to be with one another in our weakness and powerlessness, to dare to be relocated, redistributed and reconciled with ourselves, with God, with the world.

A sister poet describes it so beautifully:

> "I stand on the brink, on the edge of myself, and wonder at all that is beyond me. I am jealous of the ocean and the sky that do not seem to end, of the universe itself that holds so much immensity. I seek to comprehend all knowledge, and I cannot even know of all that has been written. I am a finite creature, but I ever struggle to hold within my grasp the mystery of being. I want the power of knowing all, of seeing all, of having all, and I cannot even possess myself. I have thoughts and fears and hopes that I often cannot

understand, nor more frequently admit. I am not a comfortable creature. Even my most cherished dreams I cannot make come true. My heart cries out to me to be God, and my life shouts out that I am not, but my faith is built on the hope that someone else is. I am left with the experience that I exist beyond myself, but I cannot contain my source. I am a grain of sand wanting to possess the ocean, and the miracle of love (of holiness), is that I can. He has made me so small so He can stretch me to immensity. He has made me so poor so He can fill me, pressed down and overflowing with His richness. He has made me so limited so that He can make me boundless. He has made me a creature so He can make me God. He has entered my heart and He has called me home."

The call to holiness is the call to discover that Jesus has made his home in you and me and one another. We are called to live and to celebrate that forever. We are called to stay shining!

9

Free for the Journey into Mature Faith

I invite you to become silent within . . . to take a moment to remember . . . to remember your own journey into maturing faith, that journey all of us continue to walk. We travel on a journey which has no roads, no paths, because each one of us walks a unique way—a journey that no one has ever walked before. As I share with you some of those moments in the lives of the people who have shared their journey with me, try to remember and to recognize your own moments.

We begin with the letter of Hebrews, the eleventh and twelfth chapters, which is the family history of all of us who claim to stand in the same faith. Only faith can guarantee the blessings that we hope for or prove the existence of the realities that at present seem unseen. It was for faith that our ancestors were commended; and, it is by faith that we understand that the world was created by one Word from God. It was because of their faith that Abel and Enoch, Noah and Abraham, and Sarah—all of these—died in faith before receiving any of the things that had been promised. Yet, they saw them in the far distance and welcomed them, recognizing that they were only strangers and nomads on earth.

People who use such terms about themselves make it quite plain that they are in search of their real homeland. They can hardly have meant the country they came from, since they had the opportunity to go back to it. In fact, they were longing for a better homeland—their heavenly homeland. That is why God is not ashamed to be called their God, since he has founded the city for them. Is there any need to say more? The prophets, these men and women whose faith conquered kingdoms, did what was right and earned their promises.

These people of faith could keep a lion's mouth shut, put out blazing fires and emerge unscathed from battle. They were weak people who were given strength to be brave in war and drive back foreign invaders. Some came back to their wives from the dead by resurrection. And others submitted to torture refusing release, so that they would rise again to a better life. Some had to bear being pilloried, flogged or even chained up in prison. They were stoned, sawed in half or beheaded. They were homeless and dressed in the skins of sheep and goats. They were penniless and given nothing but ill treatment. They were too good for the world and they went out to live in deserts and mountains and in caves and ravines. These are all heroes and heroines of faith—and, they did not receive what was promised, since God had made provision for them, for us, to have something better. And, they were not to reach perfection except with us.

And these were men and women who lived as if they saw the invisible. This then is our faith ... this is our heritage—a journey that began long before we were aware of it. Each one of us is part of that march of time, that march of faith. We are a faith family called to a new consciousness, to a new prophecy, to a new dream, a new kind of community, a new depth of faith, a new type of possibility. No longer is the faith of the anonymous multitude possible. We are called into the faith of the disciple, the witness, the apostle, and if need be, the martyr.

Faith is the spark, but God is the fire. Faith is no longer simply a content, a matter of knowledge; but faith has become more and more a decision—a decision no one can make for us. How is your faith decisive? What difference has your faith made in your life? What holds you in the faith? Why do you continue to walk in your faith community? What is the rock on which your faith is built? If everything else goes, what do you have to hang on to? What is your Gospel? Are you free for the journey into maturing faith? These are the questions I have been asking the people of our community, and I would like to share with you something of their journey as an invitation for you to recognize where your faith, your journey, your growing into that fire may lie.

What is faith?, I remember asking a young woman of our parish, raising her two children alone. I found her one day in church. She was reading the Old Testament. She had never read it before, and she never realized how much she had offended God. And, she did not know what to do. As she came into our community, one day in our catechumenate we were trying to share about what faith is today. We kept coming up with the old descriptions, the old formulas ... and, she just jumped up and said, "No. Faith is courage—the courage to continue to live when there is no reason to continue to live."

Faith is saying, "Yes," when you know what the consequences will be. Faith is saying, "yes," when you do not know what the consequences will be. Faith is to be happy in unhappy times, to have an inner security in time of insecurity, to live with the unanswered questions, the paradox, the nonsense, the absurdity.

I used to think of faith as a continuum, a step-by-step journey to perfection and greater faith. Now I know that it is by leaps and bounds, that faith is not a march onward and upward. Faith is so often filled with detours. We take four steps forward and six backward. It is getting stuck in a deep rut on the dirt road and not being able to find or see a way out of it. It is being able to smile and be glad the morning after a morbidly depressing day. It is being able to see a glimmer of light in the far, far distance. It is being satisfied with small, small advances in myself or other people ... knowing that I know nothing, yet believing that my presence does make a difference, that life would be different if I were not here.

I can say for sure that I know Jesus as a dear and close friend, and yet, I have met Him more in His little ones many times. Faith is less about dogma and laws than it is about relationship, friendship and love. Faith gives me the courage to love those who are not lovable, not attractive, even nasty. I know I would not be a person of faith today if I had not met people who were excellent role models in terms of being courageous, strong innovators in the face of opposition, hostility and, at times, apathy. Faith is a community of faith persons, who give you the strength and courage to continue on that lonely road.

Rediscovering the Eucharist was another important and major landmark in my journey in faith. It is difficult to put the different elements in order of importance because they all seem to fit naturally together, to dovetail together, to follow one on the other so that in the end, I do not know which came first. I know, I believe, that it was the grace of God that held all together, held all those people in all those places, when I needed them. It was He who drew me and attracted me to Himself and the Eucharist. He was there all the time, but I chose to ignore HIs continuing invitations until I was forced by necessity to do so. The necessity being a hunger, an emptiness, a fatigue that bread alone could not fill.

Faith is other people, especially if I cannot find even the mustard seed of my faith. Faith is picking myself up, dusting myself off, and starting all over again. Maturity of faith is accepting the fact that this falling down is not a once and for all phenomenon, but something which will happen over and over again in all situations, in all circumstances. Maturity of faith is in knowing and accepting the reality that my life is in transition—changing and moving all the time. As soon as I get settled, content, something or someone comes along to change all that, to change me. Maturity of faith is trying to see Christ in everyone and realizing that it is impossible to do it alone.

Maturity of faith is continuing to believe in the revolution, but realizing that I am the first enemy, the first one to overcome. Maturity of faith is knowing that I may not see the Prince of the revolution in my lifetime, but still being happy to continue in a hopeless cause—hopeless by worldly standards. Maturity of faith is realizing that I am getting older having little or no security in my life—that I am poor and will probably always be so. That even all that is OK. Yes, I can live with that. Yes, I can live without.

Maturity of faith is getting very upset at the Gospel reading—especially where it says, "Do not judge others, or you will be judged." ... the part about not seeing the beam in my eye and pointing out the speck in my friend's eye. Maturity of faith is believing that things can be different, can be better,

even though all signs and indications suggest otherwise. Those
are some of the spontaneous responses of our community as
we explored our readiness for the journey into maturity of
faith.

Faith today . . . what are its marks? its characteristics? Faith
today is *humble*. I think the most difficult thing for me to
learn after I went through the Gregorian University was to
learn to recognize that I did not have all the answers. We were
trained and taught well that if we did not know the answer, we
could at least confuse the questioner. We were so terribly
arrogant; we were so terribly triumphalistic. One of the great
gifts of Vatican II is of a humbleness before the mystery of
faith, of realizing how fragile it is—how terribly fragile that
gift of faith is.

Faith today is *personal*. No longer is it enough to be born
into the faith. Anyone in religious education today is very
much aware that the sacraments do not create something when
there is nothing there. So many have been baptized, yet they
have not been evangelized. And that interiorization of faith
does not come easy. Most of us were given too many answers
before we had any questions. And, how difficult it was for me
to be able to say, "I do not know." The second most difficult
thing for me to say was that I need help, that I do not have it
all together, that I am not the rugged individualist, all com-
petent person/priest I was trained to be. How freeing it has
been to recognize that each one of us is wounded and vulnerable and is a sinner. We need one another for healing and
for forgiveness.

And so that experience of faith that is so uniquely personal,
that each one of us has, that is different from one to another,
can only be fully experienced together. Each one of us has
only a fragment of the totality of what is given to us. Faith
today is personal, and yet in a new way, it is also *fraternal*—it
comes out of brotherhood and sisterhood. Perhaps most fundamental is that faith has to be *contemplative*. There is no way
of being faithful to the Gospel, there is no way of continuing
on the journey, except contemplatively. We are blessed by the
words of the men and women of great faith, who call us to a
humble faith, who call us to a new fraternal faith, who call us
to a new depth of faith, a new experience of faith.

Fr. Rene Voillaume, the founder of the Little Brothers and Little Sisters of Jesus, speaks of faith reminding us that in every Christian there is an indispensable core—an indispensable core. What a special moment it is when we begin to experience that my faith is not mine, rather faith is His gift, His faithfulness. And, the only reason why I can believe is because of His loving companion presence.

Not one of us could be reading a book such as this, could be here, if it were not because He is in each of us—at every moment breathing life into us. Each of us knows our own story of how prayer is a hunger, yet that is but the beginning of the journey. It comes into its maturity when we recognize and know that our hunger for faith is really His hunger for us. Every Christian possesses the potentiality which this gives, which we see in its fullness in the great contemplatives. The more a person finds him or herself responsible, the more that person has to find in his or her own life this intimate contact with Christ. There is no mediator between Jesus and us. Only Jesus can teach us to pray, only Jesus can teach us in faith, and it is only Jesus teaching through us that can draw others into that kind of conversion—the only faith that is radiant in the world today.

And we will have still more need of this as we are less and less protected in the world in which we live. For we live in a world that is secularized, materialistic, even when it is not explicitly atheistic. If we do not experience the tremor of atheism, than we are not people of our times. And it is into this environment that Jesus promised he will always be with us. Voillaume speaks of the bread of the Gospel and the wine of contemplation—in walking with others in faith, we shall learn to replenish our own stores of faith and of prayer. There are many ways of faith, as many as there are vocations and spiritual families, yet they all lead to the trackless desert of personal, inexpressible encounter with the Lord in silence and the gifts of the Spirit.

T.S. Eliot in his magnificent poem, "Ash Wednesday," over fifty years ago cried out, "Is there enough silence for the Word to be heard?" Is there enough silence in ourselves for the Lord to make Himself present? And one of the great temptations of people most dedicated to ministry is the temptation of ministry itself. Ministry is much easier than listening and being faithful to the journey to deeper faith.

Karl Rahner, one of the great theologians of our day, has repeatedly pointed out that the Christian of today must be contemplative or he or she ceases to be Christian. Christianity is Christ's ineffable nearness bestowing healing, forgiveness and fulness. Rahner's conviction is that there is a basic, inescapable, universally human experience of the reality we call God, one that is colored by the present day situation of people. The modern person keenly experiences the absence of God and we need an initiation, a mystagogy into this experience of God.

Are you frightened by the silence of God? Do you feel yourself in the presence of a Presence deeper than yourself? Do other people experience in us and recognize in us something that is more than our experience, education, or background? People are looking for more than me or you. Is there a mystery in our lives? Does God really fill us with awe? Do you ever tremble before the mystery of God?

Paul Tillich, the great American/Swiss theologian, a generation ago raised the question, "Who is the person who trembles before God?" Have we lost our capacity to tremble before God? There are many degrees of faith and it is so easy to content oneself with a little. Yet, our world will not let us get away with it. And that is one of the great graces of our day—thank God for the crisis, the immense and terrible problem of God. One of the core problems of our day is the immense and terrible problem of God. And so we must look more closely and rejoice in the struggles we must undergo in order to find God. And to realize that each one of us has to discover Him. No one else can discover Him for us.

None adequately possesses Him; none of us adequately believes in Him—yet. But we must have a hunger, we must know that we are on a journey. To be a Christian is to be a person of God, to be a person of the church, to realize that He is in us. We need to realize, even perhaps more embarrassingly, that it is easy to believe in God—easy to believe in Christ, easy to believe in prayer. My problem comes not with the conversion to Christ, but what Christ does to me when He takes me in and turns me to His people.

Jesus was not simply human, but Jesus chose to be a poor man. Jesus in his Incarnation has drawn us all into solidarity with the poor, with the marginal ones, with the little ones. This is the most unexpected revolution. It has already taken place. And we know what it has cost our brothers and sisters in Central America and Africa to walk that journey. Jesus said, "Where I am, I want you to be." And where is Jesus? Where are we absolutely sure of finding Him? Where did He locate Himself again and again?

Jesus has called us on a journey that none of us would ever choose to go ... a journey that the human heart will never understand. There is a kind of love that just comes out of necessity with living with other people, but faith in the person of Jesus breaks into our lives and gives us a call that we would never have chosen. So often we are not ready to hear this call. When people came to Jesus, Jesus listened very carefully. And with the first question, "What must I do to enter the kingdom?", Jesus was very gentle. "Keep the commandments." But be very careful with the second question. If you listen more carefully, there is always a second question, and the second question is always the question of revelation, of revealing who we are, who we are called to become—not just as an individual, but as a community, even as a church. And that young man, whom Jesus looked upon and loved, said, "What must I do to become mature?"

Do you really want to know? Sometimes I wish I knew a little less; sometimes I wish I did not meet certain people who ask questions of me I cannot answer, that compel me to recognize how ignorant I am and how blind we have been for so long a time.

And Jesus said, "If you want to be mature, I offer you four imperatives: sell all that you have, give it to the poor, and then maybe you will be able to come; then, only if you come that far, only then can you follow me." We try in so many ways to get out of that embarrassing, disturbing word of scripture. It is important to hold onto those special moments of scriptures when you wish you had not read it, or you wish you had slept that Sunday morning. But so often, he gets into us.

Pay attention to the Word of God you find most disturbing, most embarrassing. What is the Word of God that has haunted you half your lifetime? Jesus' words are revolutionary. There is no revolution that has ever come close to what Jesus has asked of us. Mark's gospel is child's play compared to what Christ has asked of us and what Christ has already done. He has already done it! Even so, he is asking of us.

According to Voillaume, if our hearts are not in anguish for God, if we do not hurt, then our hearts are not poor and are not attentive to the Holy Spirit. Have you ever experienced a pain for God? Did you ever feel such intense longing? If we are not in anguish for God, then indeed the church will not show its true image, and the Holy Spirit will not be able to manifest Itself. Will we be able to respond to what the Church has called us to become?

Can we move into this kind of maturity of faith? I do not believe that there is one saint who has not suffered through the Church—and that is normal. The Church—that is the multitude, that faith that we have, that minimal faith. Again we are called. Again and again, we find a line in the Gospel, "And the disciples believed in Him." And the disciples believed in Him—again and again, there was a continual deepening of faith.

In Paul, we see this most explicitly—how Paul became more and more radical. He cried out, when he was struck to the ground on the road to Damascus, "Who are you?" And the voice came back, "I am Jesus whom you are oppressing." All of us are oppressors, all of us—even though we do not know it and there is no personal sin involved. Yet, in some way, we are oppressors. Perhaps we are more comfortable with the title "sin"; we are more at home being sinners. We do not like to be called oppressors. Still, we are—we have been for a long time. And only faith—human love is not enough—only faith can bring us beyond that, can call us into a kind of solidarity—the solidarity that used to be called mercy, then charity, then commitment. Now, the word is solidarity—becoming one—not simply with Jesus, but to catch up with Jesus where Jesus is. "Where I am, I want you to be." And, Jesus is always with the oppressed.

No two people on earth live the Gospel the same way. The deeper the Gospel permeates our life and being, the more personal form it assumes. What is the rock of your faith? For me, it was the Eucharist. And, I thought I understood the Eucharist. Now, I know much more clearly that Jesus, in giving us Eucharist, was trying to help us recognize His body and blood. That is the Incarnation, He identified Himself with every man, with every child, with every woman.

Recently, a man stopped me and asked, "What is the faith of a mustard seed?" I had never heard that question before. I pondered for a moment—the smallest particle of faith—how much is that? I think we have to put that into the context of life. How significant is the smallest particle of life? To believe means to experience the presence of God in our life in such a way that we choose, that we make a decision. And the gap between non-faith and non-life and an act of faith—no longer is it adequate to recite a formula of faith, to make an act of faith in terms of a verbal formula. Today, it is the question of when did I believe today? When did I hope? When did I love?

It used to be easy for me to pray, because in my prayer I realized that Jesus and I are the same temperament. He understands me ... He is in my image and likeness. I found it very easy in the seminary to be faithful to prayer. What a different experience going into a parish where people do not care what degrees you have, nor will they be likely to read any of the books you have written. And they ask different kinds of questions ... or they do not even ask questions—yet, they survive because of a level of faith in their lives, a level of faith that often humbles me.

One of the most haunting lines of the liturgy—after we have prayed the Lord's Prayer, is a short prayer. We say, "Look not upon our sins, but on the faith of the Church." I have come to understand or, in some way, to sense more and more deeply what is the faith of the Church, the Church that has handed down that incredible journey of 2,000 years right on to today—something more than faith in God, faith in myself, faith in scripture, even perhaps, more than faith in the Eucharist ... that there is something very special about a Catholic's faith, a universal faith.

Remember the film, "O God," and that magnificent line where John Denver confronted his wife, the believer in the family. He said to her, "I thought you believed in God?" And she replied, "I believe in God, but I never thought He really existed." How easy it has been to say, I believe—never to expect His immediate presence in my life in such a way that I can no longer act except as one seeing the invisible. It is so easy to fall back into oneself. It is only faith that compels us to move beyond ourselves.

When the disciples wanted to embrace Jesus, when Jesus asked them, "Do you love me?" He did not say, hold me and embrace me. He said, "Feed my lambs, feed my sheep. Give them something to eat." If we could only believe the truth, if we could only believe what we write, if we could only believe what we teach. Are you ever embarrassed at what you teach? Do you ever get embarrassed by what you proclaim so beautifully? How many leaps of faith we have taken in these last decades. Keep on practicing your highjumping! We are only beginning!

In Baptism, the Christian community asks us, "What do you ask of the Church?" We respond, "*Faith*". Did you realize what you were letting yourself in for? Faith is attention to the living presence of God in the depths of our being compelling us to move out of ourselves, to go and to make disciples, to make the world His. The most incredible expression of Vatican II is that we are a sacrament of the liberation, of the sanctification, of the salvation, of the world. The seven sacraments are for those who believe. But for the world, the fundamental sacrament is each one of us together believing—not my faith, but the faith of He who holds us together. And the very fact that we believe is the greatest evidence of His loving companion presence with us.

So our faith today is humble ... it is fragile ... it is personal ... it is fraternal ... it is contemplative ... it is evangelical. It is prophetic, in the sense that when I begin to experience His presence in me, the sign that I believe is that I can no longer hold it within myself. I am compelled to share it with others. My life cannot remain the same. And, the more I choose to live these ways-of-faith through my words, my thoughts, my

actions, the freer I shall be for the journey into maturing faith.
In his letter to the Romans, Paul describes his journey into
maturing faith ... our journey:

> "Therefore, since we are justified by faith, we have peace
> with God through our Lord, Jesus Christ. Through him we
> have obtained access to this grace in which we stand, and
> we rejoice in our hope of sharing the glory of God. More
> than that, we rejoice in our sufferings, knowing that suf-
> fering produces endurance, and endurance produces
> character, and character produces hope, and hope does not
> disappoint us, because God's love has been poured into our
> hearts through the Holy Spirit which has been given to
> us." (Rom 5:1-5)

10

Free to Dream the Dream of Jesus

Where there is no vision, people become demoralized and perish; they become lost. Workers do not know why they are working; parents forget why they are sacrificing for their children; young people question what it is they are preparing for. Yet, we do not need to be without vision. Jesus shares his vision with us. he wants us to see ourselves and our world as he sees us—as we are, as we could be. When we pray, Jesus lights his light in us so we can see. He lets us dream his dream. What Jesus dreams in us is the Kingdom of God. When we share his vision, it becomes for us a presence, a power and a promise.

As *presence*, Jesus' dream concerns God's indwelling with us, his knowledge of us, his deep, abiding, unconditional love for us. The Lord lights His light in us and draws us into that presence which is Himself within each of us. This is especially evident in the prayer He prays in us—praying that His spirit will give us the power for our unknown self, our unknown vision, to grow strong. To pray is to be aware of the prayer that Jesus prays for each of us and to wonder at the vision that is unfolding, revealing itself within us. "I am with you always. I am praying for you. I will give you a new spirit." And where the spirit of the Lord is, there is freedom. And we with our unveiled faces, reflecting like mirrors the brightness of the Lord, all grow brighter and brighter as we are turned into the image, the vision that we reflect.

As *power*, we see that through us, the Father goes on

working. "I have come to cast fire on the earth. You are that fire and I would that you enkindle the world. Do not worry, do not be afraid." The most repeated words of Jesus are, "I forbid you to be afraid." Jesus' power in us precludes fear. In fact, Jesus predicted far greater things of us than he did of himself. "Greater things than these will you do." He began his ministry with, "I am the light of the world;" he concluded it with, "You are the light of the world; you are the salt of the earth." He dared to give us commands which would be utterly absurd unless they were revelations of a new power at work in us far beyond anything we could wish or imagine.

And as *promise*, we discover that in Christ we are a new creation bound for better things. "I have given to you the glory that the Father has given to me. Where I am, I want you to be."

Whether it is called a vision, a dream or an insight, we share in the seeing and we are part of the vision. We are both the see-ers and the seen. Because we are the vision of Jesus, because we are the Kingdom, Jesus wants, he needs to communicate his vision to us.

We have all experienced many different moments of the vision; we occasionally see who we are and where we are going. Yet at other times, we lose the sight. Perhaps the most sober words on the importance of vision are found in Matthew's passage on the Sermon on the Mount. He writes,

> "If your eye, your vision, is sound, your whole body will be filled with light; but if your eye, your vision, is impaired, not functioning, your whole body will be all darkness. Then the light inside you is darkness."

Human vision, unaided, is so small.

> "Eye has not seen, nor ear heard, nor has it entered the hearts of men or women what God is preparing for those who love him."

The light of Jesus' vision can carry us forward a long way. Elijah went on the strength of his vision for forty days and nights—all the way to Horeb, the Mount of God. So can all of us because the Lord promised,

> "I will pour out my spirit upon all mankind; young men shall see visions and old men shall dream dreams, and on my servants and handmaids I will pour a portion of my spirit." (Ac 2:17-18; Jl 3:1-2)

Yet the vision makes demands.

> "Write down the vision clearly on the tablets so that one can read it readily, for the vision still has its time; it presses on to fulfillment, it will not disappoint. If the vision delays, wait for it. It will surely come; it will not be late." (cf. Rev 1:19; 22:6-7)

All of Jesus' vision is ultimately the mystery that God is Father. No one else has my vision, my particular way of seeing what Jesus sees, nor do I know your vision, that which Jesus dreams in you, sees in you. We rarely know from whence it comes or how, only that it is there.

During a retreat, one woman shared the only remembered dream she had had where Jesus was clearly present. This simple dream came at a time, she said, of "spiritual gluttony," a time when she desired only to be alone in prayer, away from the pain of the world.

> "I was climbing a mountain road all alone with only one aim—to reach the summit. There seemed to be no particular obstacles along the way—as if I had encountered them all and gone beyond them. I made my way up, up, up. Nearing the top of this mountain, I saw higher peaks in the distance and I wished, and almost believed, I could leap from peak to peak.
>
> Then, as I came over the last rise, already sensing the exhilaration of 'having made it,' there stood a man with arms outstretched, scars on His hands, looking at me with love and understanding, with compassion and deep yearning. He said not a word, but pointed one hand toward the valley below. Then, I heard in my heart's ear, 'If you love

me, feed my sheep.' I could but melt, yield and hide my head in shame. Yet he would not let me hide my head for long; forgiveness was mine before I could utter my confession of pride, vanity and hardness of heart. I shall always remember Him smiling as I turned away and began the journey down."

She continued,

"A journey that has led me into prisons, nursing homes, mental institutions, has compelled me to relocate and to live among the poor ... a journey that Jesus continues to dream in me, a journey that has brought more peace, joy, assurance, gratitude and love than I could ever have known on the mountaintop of spiritual isolation. Finally, it is a journey into community—into sharing Jesus' dream in me with his dream in others."

Thus, we need to reflect with one another, to stir up the grace which is within us, to call to mind the vision lying latent there. Where do we get the first inklings of this vision? My first experience of the vision was seeing the faith of my father and mother. The first evangelization is in the family. The wonderful annunciation, as powerful as that of Gabriel, comes from the lips of the father and mother to the inquiring child. "The Lord is with you."

All of us remember the experience of asking the first questions about our history, the tradition of our family, the wonder of "Where have I come from?" We recall the awe of discovering the story of how we were baptized long before we became conscious. In Baptism we became holy. We were consecrated to God, to the indwelling of the Father, Son and Spirit, to the presence, power and promise. We became God's son or daughter, and His heir. We are united forever to Jesus. In some way we were plunged into Him and He into us. He has come to us and makes His home in us.

What a holy moment when a child hears the Good News, the wonderful story of his or her birth in Christ and of belonging to God's family! What a marvelous moment to know one is a temple of God in the presence of Christ; that I live now, not I, but Jesus lives in me! And what an amazing grace to be born into a Christian family, in a divine milieu, where the vision of Jesus radiates unconsciously through good people, the faithful ones who, like Anna and Simeon, Simon and Veronica, keep the vision alive.

The primary witnesses of the Gospel are not writers, not theologians, but those who live and make visible the vision of Christ within themselves. The experience of God as real is easy to know when one's family and the people of the neighborhood radiate the gifts of the Spirit—the gifts of joy, love, peace, patience, kindness, gratitude, fidelity, generosity. In their prayer we sense a force which is almost tangible, of being drawn into goodness by the power of those who believe.

And when a family, which carries the mystery of Jesus in its mind and heart, gathers around the altar, the child becomes aware of the sign of Christ's ministry—the crucifix. In the church building, in the sacramentals, in gestures like the Sign of the Cross by which we commit ourselves to live that cross, to carry it, the child learns about the commitment involved in carrying on the vision, that to be Christian, a dreamer with Jesus, each must deliberately choose Jesus. The child inwardly comes to know that at the heart of Christianity is a cross, the sign of a love on to death and beyond into resurrection. And to embrace Jesus is to embrace the Cross—to carry the Cross for oneself, for others, for the world, to become poor enough, small enough, to enter by the narrow gate of the Cross.

The vision of Jesus is activated when the child prepares for First Communion. No longer is it simply Jesus in me. In the Eucharist, we are drawn by a kinship of grace into a community. "Where two or three are gathered together in my name," there lives a community in the mystery of Jesus. The experience of being confirmed by a bishop renews the call of the disciples to go and bring forth fruit. And we perceive the vision of Jesus in the sacraments of reconciliation and anointing, as well as in the seeking and searching into vocation.

Every sacrament embraces a vision, a remembrance so deep, so intense, that Christ is compelled to render himself present. A sacrament is a prophecy, a future, a promise; it is the Lord. My Lord and my God!

The mystery of Jesus is essentially His Word, His Word heard, received deeply within oneself, to be pondered. The Scriptures reveal the vision of Jesus. It is that Word, taken into contemplation, that transforms us so that we become fire upon the earth.

That Word is often discovered in silence and in prayer. We need silence in which to dream; we need prayer to receive the vision. We are always losing the vision, yet it can never be really lost. It haunts us, clings to us, finds us again and again. In Christ there is always new creation, new bread, our daily Bread, our daily surprise and wonder, our new vision and dream and faith.

Thus, we first become aware of this vision within us from our families, from our experience of Church and sacraments, and from diving into the Scriptures. Our vision grows like a mustard seed. Our dream embraces the radical dimensions of Jesus' dream.

In the vision of Jesus, the poor reign with God, the sorrowing are consoled, the meek inherit the earth, the hungry and thirsty are filled, the single-hearted see God, the peacemakers are called the sons and daughters of God. Who could be so inventive as to dream the Beatitudes alone?

In the vision of Jesus, anyone who brings his or her gift to the altar and recalls that a sister or a brother has a complaint, leaves the gift and goes first to be reconciled.

In the vision of Jesus, you offer no resistance to injury. If anyone presses you for one mile, you go two. You love your enemy and pray for those who persecute you. When the hour comes, you will be given what to say; the spirit of your Father will be speaking in you. Your soul will find rest.

In the vision of Jesus, lepers are made whole, paralytics walk, the blind see, captives are set free, the poor have the gospel preached to them.

In the vision of Jesus, you do not worry about your livelihood, what you are to eat or to drink; you ask and you receive. You have courage; your sins are forgiven. You know that you are loved. Because of your faith, because of your vision, it is done to you.

The questions of Jesus are an inexhaustible revelation of his dream. "Who do you say that I am? Do you love me? What do you want me to do for you? Do you want to be healed? Do you believe me? Do you dream? Did I not assure you that if you believed you would see the glory of God?"

What did Jesus see in Peter, or James, or John or Mary Magdalene? What does Jesus see in any one of us? Over and over again, the Gospel says that Jesus knew what was in their hearts. We can be absolutely sure of but one thing: that He knows us. He knows us as we do not know ourselves. What is even more important, He loves us as we cannot love ourselves, as we are worth being loved. Only Jesus has that power; He can read our depths and our heights.

Jesus could look at Peter and say, "You are Peter and upon this rock I will build my Church." Incredible! Imagine Jesus saying to you, "You are the one upon whom I will build my Church." Unbelievable as it sounds, that is what He is saying. "Upon your marriage, upon your love for one another, I will build my community."

Jesus could make wild statements about his followers, not because He was an unrealistic dreamer, but because He knows more than anyone else about the power of love. Only love creates vision; without love, there is no vision, only despair. His own heart is the power which releases in the world the tremendous reality that death no longer has any power over us.

No one knows more deeply than Jesus how much we are sinners, how much of us remains unredeemed. No one knows more deeply the reality of sin, our own personal sin, because He absorbed all of our sin into Himself and overcame it. That is why He has the right to love us and to have His vision for each of us.

Yet when do we begin to really understand this dream? Where do we start to unravel the dream of Jesus, His dream of revealing God to us as Father, His dream of us, His dream of the Holy Spirit in us?" In the Eucharist, that is where.

The ultimate vision of Jesus is Eucharist. "This is my Body." Over the broken world each day, over each newspaper, over every television newscast, we can hear with our hearts the words, "This is my Body. this is my Blood, shed, given for you." Eucharist is His vision of us, His dream for us, the gift of loving one another as He loves us. When we do this we do what He has done for us.

What would we dare to ask anyone to do in remembrance of us? Jesus dares to ask us to become His presence, His vision, His healing. What He calls us to do is to put ourselves aside, to live in and out of him. "Live in me and I shall live in you." And he reminds us, "Unless you take up the vision and come after me . . ." The Eucharist, then, is what fully reveals and nourishes this vision of Jesus. It is the basis of our insatiable hope.

The Eucharist tells each of us who we are. In it Jesus calls us by name. He asks the question, "Who are you looking for?" over and over, until we hear our own answer. That is the same question he asked Magdalene in the garden. And he waits until we answer, "It is the Lord!"

How often faith bursts within us like a flame and we do not recognize it. What matters is that Jesus recognizes us for who we are. He recognizes us even when we do not know ourselves and He continues to come, day in and day out. "Behold I stand at the door and knock." And he will always be knocking. "If anyone opens the door, I will come in and I will dine with that one."

No one else dreams our dreams or has our vision. There is in all of us a hidden, unknown dream. The first and ultimate scene of our dream is "Abba—Father." God has sent into our hearts the spirit of the Son who cries out "Abba" and gives us an identity, tells us who and whose we are. Everyone has learned to dream in a special way that mysterious dream that dwells in each one of us. We cannot control our dreams and they continue in us during all of our lives. Perhaps this is the great sign of whose we are—when we dream the dream of our Father, when we dream the dream of Jesus.

No one can ever behold the vision that I have. Everyone sees God in a unique and unrepeatable way. In each of us there is an unknown vision, an unknown faith, that the whole world is in need of.

> "The secret of the Kingdom of God is given to you; to you the mystery of the reign of God has been confided." (cf. Mk 4:11a; Mt 13:11a)

Our vision remains partial, incomplete, and this is a special kind of poverty—even in the vision of the Church, the Christian vision. We do not know where it comes from, we do not know how it comes—it is just there. Each one of us is beginning to realize that the vision is not something which is ours alone. By ourselves, we lose it, forget it. Only together can we remember it and allow it to unfold. The vision completes us and enables us to go out of ourselves. Our dreams extend us beyond ourselves ... and into community.

The Christian knows that his or her vision is personal and yet is not a vision to be lived in isolation. The inception, development and transmission of the Christian vision is always an experience with others. We dream because of the people who dream, because of the One who has come and lives in our midst, even though we do not readily recognize Him. We discover the vision which has been imprinted deep within our hearts. We have been given the Holy Spirit in order to recognize the vision of Jesus which we have already received. And the Spirit helps us to recognize this vision. The Spirit makes intercession for us with groanings beyond the human word. The Christian dares to dream, to carry the vision, because of Something, Someone, living and breathing in our lives!

Realizing Jesus' vision being dreamed in us is bound to change us. I change and I enter a new level of presence as I dream. I am transformed by my concept of myself, by my dream, by my reach. Although the vision is within ourselves, never before have we experienced a goal so far beyond us, so challenging to us. Human vision itself is inexhaustible, creative and joyful. We are the image of God in our capacity for self-awareness.

Imagine the dream God has—a dream so real that it became creation, a love so immense that it became Incarnation. Imagine Jesus' dream, what he sees in us. In Christ, we are dreamers and co-dreamers. We dream together with him. He dreams in us, creating a new world.

Re-vision is a consequence of being in Christ. We are each continually redefining our vision beyond our own fragile human sight. "A new prophecy, a new commandment I give you. Love one another." He asks us to, "Live on in my love. You will suffer in the world but take courage." We work and suffer impelled by that energy of His which is so powerful a force in us.

> "I have come that you may have life, that you may have the real vision of life." (cf. Jn 10:10b; 12:46)

That vision is a remembrance of the past and a promise of the future, that which was and that which is to come. John's Gospel is his vision. "In the beginning was the Word, in the beginning was the vision." In effect it says, "I, John, see a new vision." Each of us must be able to do likewise, to see a new vision. Each one of us must put our name there—I, Edward; I, Mary; I, Peter; I, Susan—I see a new vision. Each of us is a Book of Revelation. Each of us is a book not only of the past but of the future.

Nothing can determine the future except faith, no one has the power to create the future so totally as the person of faith. Faith or vision is the ability to remember the future. What a paradox! To look back at Jesus is the same thing as looking forward to all we can be. What power! "You do not yet know what you are to become." (cf. 1 Jn 3:2)

We can remember the future because Jesus lets his prophecy overshadow us in the Eucharist. In every Eucharist he dares to say,

> "I abandon myself into your hands. Do with me what you will. Whatever you may do, I thank you. I am ready for all, I accept all, Let only your will be done in me, and in all your creatures; I wish no more than this, my friends.

> Into your hands I commend my soul. I offer it to you with all the love of my heart. For I love you my sister, my brother, and so need to give myself, to surrender myself into your hands without reserve and with boundless confidence. For you are my friends."

Jesus gives himself to us over and over. Can we receive Him?

In rediscovering Jesus' prophecy, we re-vision our own life to be a labor of pain until Christ is formed. Even now, I find myself enjoying the sufferings I endure for Him in my flesh. I fill up what is lacking in His sufferings for the sake of His Body, the Church.

There is no redemption except through the Cross. I think one of the greatest acts of faith in Scripture is that of the good thief dying next to a deserted, beaten man who could not save himself. That thief could turn to the wounded figure and say, "Lord, remember me when you come into your Kingdom." His faith, his vision, rewarded him with the words, "This day you will be with me in the Kingdom." Each day we too can be with Jesus in the Kingdom because the Kingdom of heaven is within us.

Yet human nature being what it is, we find it hard to accept the vision of Jesus. We do not know how to respond to a vision, to a God who is so poor he takes on the weakness of men and women, who calls us to share a vision which is risky and may cost us our life, to a dream that demands a new kind of presence, a new depth of love. The radical vision to which Jesus calls seems far off because we are still wounded, broken, fragmented. Because of the gospel, we know how irresistible and powerful Jesus' vision is, and that only serves to make us very cautious.

The self-awareness of Jesus is a vision of love. It is simply a revelation of His love. No one can ever be as totally human as Jesus was. No human love exists as intensely as His. What He calls us to do is to put ourselves aside to live in Him and out of Him. "Live in me and I shall live in you." He calls us to live out of His power, His grace, His love.

Yet we are not convinced that Jesus loves us and that it is this love which redeems us. We are not yet sure that we have the power in our hands and in our hearts. We are still hoping that there is an easier way, that we can somehow receive the Eucharist without being burned, scorched, broken, consumed ... without becoming Eucharist ourselves to be broken and given out to others.

Eucharist teaches us to accept the presence of someone not myself, the very giver of the being that I am. Ezra writes,

"In the innermost depth of man's being, God is making himself known in an unutterable pulsation of love, the presence of an animating heart, a cosmic pulsation, a heart which answers my own, a divine heart animating the cosmic immensity of a life flow."

And Eucharist, the praying church, is the pulsating heart of the universe. This mystery of the praying church opens up a new experience of God, of ourselves. The praying church is an ocean, we are the shore. Each day we are invited to beachcomb for the new gift which we are given. What incredible communion with divine life! "Do this in memory of me." Dream my dream!

Even so, we each prefer a certain amount of darkness to the fullness of the light of Jesus' vision. We are not yet ready for the truth; yet we feel the responsibility as the vision continues to haunt us. "You are the light of the world," it keeps repeating. If our world is dark, if our city has no hope, then it is because we, who have been given the light, have believed more in the power of darkness than in the power of light.

The Gospel of John most fully expresses Jesus' vision when he talks about His own experience of knowing the Father:

"Eternal life is this: to know you, the only true God, and Jesus Christ whom you have sent. I have made your name known; I have made your Kingdom known to them, and will continue to make it known so that the love with which you love me may be in them and so that I may be in them."

(Jn 17:3, 26)

The vision of Jesus is real. If only we could believe the truth—that we are in Him and that He is in us! "If you but knew the gift of God and who it is that lives in you, that speaks in you, that dreams in you!" All that Jesus has learned from the Father is given to us, and so he calls us His friends. "As the Father has loved me, so I have loved you; as the Father has sent me, so I also send you. As the Father has dreamed his dream in me, so I dream my dream in you."

And so Jesus, day in and day out, continues to offer this vision to us, imploring us to rise to the challenge, until someday perhaps, we shall be free enough to abandon ourselves into Jesus' hands, to dream His dream. Others will then be able to say of us, "It is the Lord." And Jesus will say to us, "It is Myself!" And we shall say with Paul, "I live now, not I, but YOU live in me!" (Gal 2:20)

> Blessed be God the Father of our Lord Jesus Christ,
> Who has blessed us with all the spiritual blessings
>   of the cosmos in Christ.
> Before the world was made, He chose us,
>   chose us in Christ to be whole, holy and
>   without sin and to live through love in
>   His presence.
> Determining that we should become His adopted
>   sons and daughters through Christ,
> He has let us know the mystery of His purpose,
>   the hidden plan He so kindly made in Christ
>   from the beginning
> To act upon when the times had run their course
>   to the end;
> That he would bring everything together under
>   Christ, as head,
> Everything in the heavens, the cosmos, and
>   everything on earth,
>   And now, you too in Him! (Eph 1:3-11a)

Postscript

About the Author

Fr. Edward J. Farrell is a versatile priest with deep pastoral commitments. He did graduate work in the classics (University of Michigan), in theology (Gregorian University, Rome) and in psychology (University of Detroit).

He is widely respected as a lecturer and writer, whose books and tapes are read and heard all over the English-speaking world. Since 1978 he has been pastor of St. Agnes Parish in Detroit. Among his many publications are *Prayer Is a Hunger, Surprised By the Spirit, Disciples and Other Strangers,* and *Can You Drink This Cup.*

On the Thirtieth Anniversary of the Author's Ordination

Lord, if I take the years
    and pour them in some common cup
    need they be lifted once again?
I have already struck the rock in faith;
    Where flows the water is not mine to see.
    You faulted Moses for his hesitation,
                 — ours is life long.
    Yet, I do believe these bones will sing at Horeb,
        in the land you gave my fathers long ago.
Already, at evening, I can hear
    the chanting echo like the hooves of distant horsemen coming.
To listen takes such stillness
    and the heart, as always, plays the lone, loud drummer.

I've walked world-wide,
    preached the Word from East to West.
I feel I've been your shuttle, Lord,
    carrying the cup till even that has cracked.
Your word,
    read in every time zone
    bears the soil and smear of all men's race and tongue.
Pages worn.
    Is it not time you blessed the dusty, aching feet
        of one who preached the Gospel?
Spent,
    I take my shoes off at the holy ground.
The younger deer fleet-footed go upon the mountain tops.
They breathe still the thinner air.
    I seek your mysteries quietly now, in the evening,
by the fires of your tents.
    Draw back the veils and show me
the precious starlight of the long, dark skies.

We make our missions when we're young,
    thinking them needed; valiantly we spend our powers

not knowing till the shadows fall
     there was no need.
It was our weakness opened doors once closed to armies
    and the battering rams.
The quiet words,
    the human sharing among other friends
these moved the mountains, parted seas with clarity.
(I thought the dry bed just another road.)

Ordained in childhood by desire, by all these years' annointing
    now I am your priest.
Much as the water added to the wine is seen no more
or the burnt incense mingles till it's breathed as air,
so I, by mingling in You, Christ, the Priest,
    no longer am, but in You have my being.
until there shall be one Christ,
     loving Himself.
    Omega, Thou, my life's begun.

                   Barbara Donohue